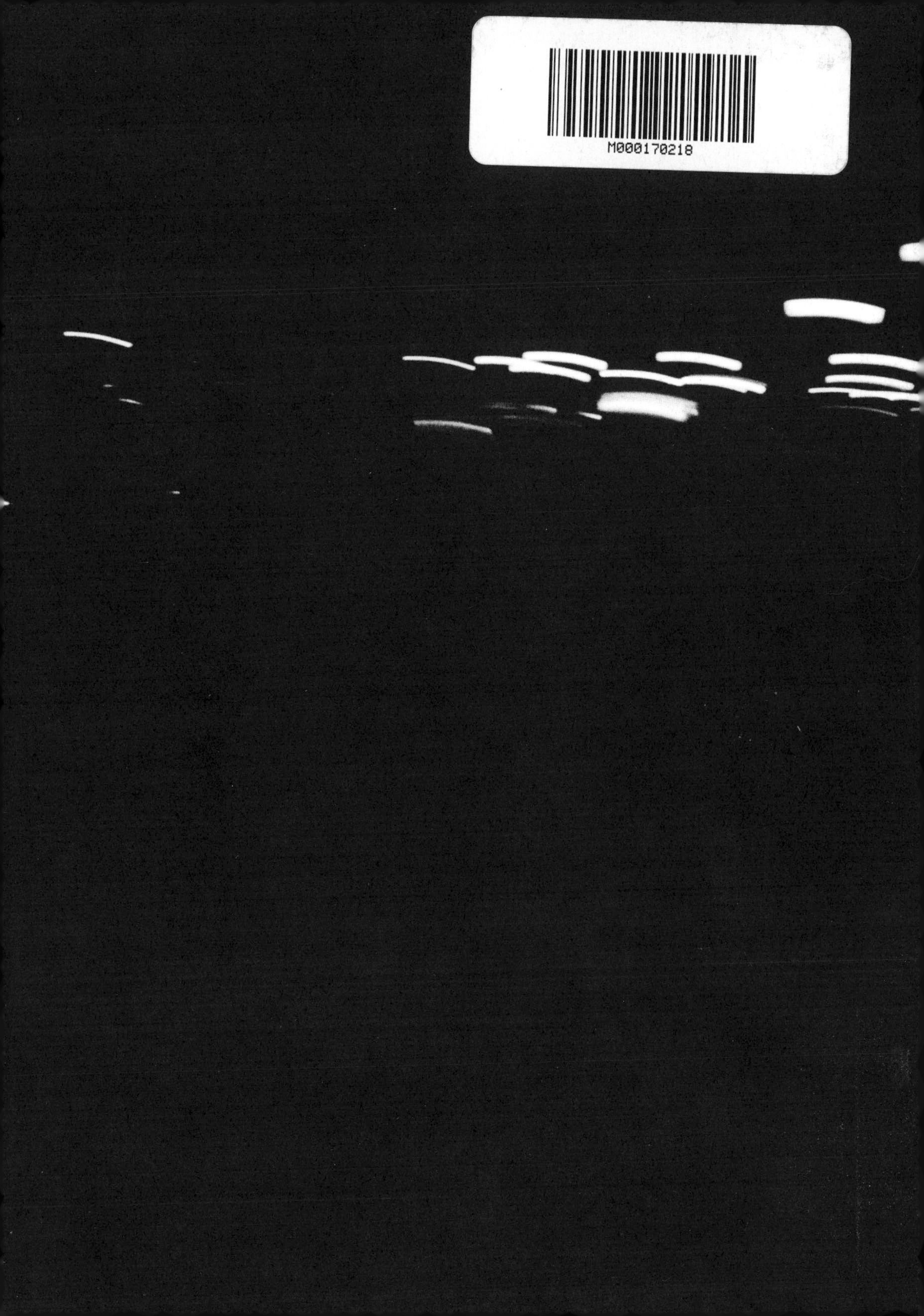

THE
LIFE

STEVE MCQUEEN

THE LIFE

STEVE MCQUEEN

DWIGHT JON ZIMMERMAN

© 2017 Quarto Publishing Group USA Inc.

First published in 2017 by Motorbooks, an imprint of Quarto Publishing Group USA Inc., 401 Second Avenue North, Suite 310, Minneapolis, MN 55401 USA. Telephone: (612) 344-8100 Fax: (612) 344-8692

www.QuartoKnows.com

Motorbooks titles are also available at discounts in bulk quantity for industrial or sales-promotional use. For details contact the Special Sales Manager by email at specialsales@quarto.com or by mail at The Quarto Group., 401 Second Avenue North, Suite 310, Minneapolis, MN 55401 USA

10 9 8 7 6 5 4 3 2 1

ISBN: 978-0-7603-5811-5

Names: Zimmerman, Dwight Jon author.
Title: The life McQueen / Dwight Jon Zimmerman.
Description: Minneapolls : Motorbooks, 2017.
Identifiers: LCCN 2017038746 | ISBN 9780760358115 (hardback)
Subjects: LCSH: McQueen, Steve, 1930-1980. | Actors--United
    States--Biography. | BISAC: BIOGRAPHY & AUTOBIOGRAPHY /
Entertainment &
    Performing Arts. | BIOGRAPHY & AUTOBIOGRAPHY / Rich &
Famous.
Classification: LCC PN2287.M547 Z56 2017 | DDC 791.4302/8092
[B] --dc23
LC record available at https://lccn.loc.gov/2017038746

Acquiring Editor: Zack Miller
Project Manager: Alyssa Bluhm
Cover and page design: Laura Drew
Page layout: Laura Drew and Beth Middleworth

Front cover photo: William Claxton
Back cover photo: Pictorial Press Ltd./Alamy Stock Photo

Printed in Canada

CONTENTS

ROOTS OF THE LEGEND

THE FOREVER "KING OF COOL"

A person is very much shaped by his environment and upbringing, and in Steve McQueen's case, the combination of parental abandonment and economic hardship created a man tough on the outside and vulnerable inside—driven to succeed, and on his terms. And he did.

McQueen was a complex individual full of contradictions: a man reaching out for intimacy but suspicious whenever he found it, demanding trust but rarely reciprocating it. Devoted father, serial cheater. A hedonist who became devout, not because he was dying, but because he truly found God. His success on the silver screen and on the racetrack and off-road propelled him above A-list stardom to hold the unique position of the "King of Cool," an icon who was as comfortable in tailored suits and expensive casual dress and manicured fingernails as he was in jeans, a T-shirt, and work boots with grease under his fingernails. Yet even at the peak of his fame and fortune, he was constantly nagged by feelings of inferiority and a fear of poverty.

Success in acting gave him the freedom to lead the life he wanted, and what he wanted with equal passion was to race and be respected by his fellow racers. He said, "An actor is a puppet, manipulated by a dozen other people. Auto racing has dignity."

A man constantly in the public eye, he was a loner, happiest by himself on a motorcycle in the desert. In *On Any Sunday*, the motorcycle racing documentary he financed and starred in, he said, "Every time I start thinking of the world as all bad, then I start seeing some people out here having a good time on motorcycles—it makes me take another look." It was a good time that motorcycling repaid him. In 1976, he was inducted into the Off-Road Motorsports Hall of Fame, and in 1999, the American Motorcycle Association inducted him into the Motorcycle Hall of Fame.

As this is written, thirty-seven years have passed since his tragic death of cancer at age fifty. Yet his influence continues to be felt on the screen and in fashion.

Biographer William F. Nolan wrote, "Steve McQueen ended as he began, a rebel outside the establishment, a man who had preserved his fierce sense of unwavering integrity against all odds, who had gone through the fire, and who had found, at the end, a deep personal peace within himself."

THE UGLY EARLY YEARS

Everyone starts somewhere. For Terrence Steven McQueen, that somewhere was Slater, Missouri, in 1930, just as the Great Depression was entering its worst years. Abandoned by his father, Terrence McQueen, when he was six months old, and then by his mother, Jullian Crawford McQueen, to relatives, when she took him back at age nine and left with him to live in California with the latest of her husbands, the seeds of angry rebellion had been deeply sown.

Not long after settling down in Los Angeles, Jullian found herself caught between an abusive husband and an out-of-control son who had become a member of a street gang. In desperation, she signed a court order that sent the delinquent McQueen to the California Junior Boys Republic, which he entered on February 6, 1945. It was there that he finally got the guidance he needed and developed a positive sense of self-worth.

As for why he kept returning to the Boys Republic after he had

become a star, McQueen said, "Because I owe the place. And you pay your debts. They tell me I do a lot of good here. And maybe I do. But lemme tell ya. . . . If I thought I'd help just one kid who was headed the way I was headed—helped him get straight with the world—that would make all the trips okay. Just one kid. You've got to give back, you can't take. And at Chino, I'm givin' back a little is all."

On April 21, 1983, in a ceremony attended by McQueen's son, Chad, and some close friends and civic officials and guests, the Steve McQueen Activity Center was dedicated. Its plaque reads,

Steve McQueen came here as a troubled boy but left here as a man. He went on to achieve stardom in motion pictures but returned to this campus often to share of himself and his fortune. His legacy is hope and inspiration to those students here now, and those yet to come.

JULLIAN CRAWFORD MCQUEEN

The first woman in McQueen's life was his mother, Jullian Crawford McQueen. A spoiled, rebellious only child, she was anything but a good mother. Blonde, blue-eyed, and beautiful, she wanted nothing less than a handsome man to show her a good time. Bored by her strict church upbringing in small-town Slater, Missouri, she ran away at sixteen to find good times and good men in the metropolis of Indianapolis.

A fling with dashing and romantic barnstorming stunt pilot Terrence William "Bill" McQueen soon found Jullian pregnant. With an uncharacteristic streak of gallantry, Bill decided to make an "honest woman" of the girl he had gotten into trouble and married her. After his birth, Bill named his son Terrence Steven. McQueen later said, "My father named me after a one-armed bookie pal of his, Steve Hall. He must have had a weird sense of humor." It was the only thing he gave Steve. Six months after Steve was born, Bill walked out of his wife and son's life, and they never saw him again.

Emotionally incapable of handling the responsibilities of motherhood,

and equally irresponsible in her choices of husbands, Jullian would drift in and out of marriages and in and out of McQueen's life.

After McQueen became successful, he took care of her, setting her up with her own business and regularly sending her checks. Though he let her back into his life for the sake of his kids, Terry and Chad, he kept his mother at arm's length. Over the years, she attempted to reconcile with her son, but too much damage had been done. In October 1965, during the shooting

> "I LEFT HOME AT THE AGE OF FIFTEEN BECAUSE THERE REALLY WAS NO HOME. . . . I HAVE HAD NO EDUCATION. I CAME FROM A WORLD OF BRUTE FORCE."
>
> —STEVE MCQUEEN

of *Nevada Smith*, McQueen received word that Jullian had suffered a cerebral hemorrhage and was in the hospital. Production was halted so he could be at her side.

At her bedside, all the pent-up pain, rage, and angst came out, and he hoped that she would recover at least enough for them to finally have the long-overdue talk. But it was not to be. On October 15, 1965, his mother died, having never recovered consciousness.

At the gravesite, the only attendants were McQueen and his family and two close friends, publicist David Foster and Foster's wife, Jackie. McQueen began a brief eulogy and then began to cry, unable to finish. It was a moment when Foster felt that McQueen "was a lost soul."

THE REBEL BECOMES ONE OF "THE FEW"

In 1947, after a recruitment poster caught his eye, McQueen joined the United States Marine Corps. Following boot camp, Private First Class McQueen was assigned as a tank engine mechanic in the Second Division, Fleet Marine Force, and stationed at Camp Lejeune, North Carolina.

McQueen still had much of his rebel past in him. "I was busted back down to private about seven times," he admitted. "The only way I could have made corporal was if all the other privates in the marines dropped dead." He also did time in the brig for going AWOL. As it turned out, that real-life experience would serve him well as Captain Virgil Hilts, the Cooler King, in *The Great Escape*.

McQueen redeemed himself in 1948 during a training exercise in the Arctic. A transport ship he was aboard hit a sandbank, causing tanks and marines to be tossed into the icy waters. McQueen personally rescued a five-man tank crew. In recognition for his heroic action, McQueen was assigned to the Honor Guard protecting the presidential yacht.

In 1950, McQueen was honorably discharged. "The marines gave me discipline I could live with," he said. "By the time I got out, I was able to cope with things on a more realistic level. All in all, despite my problems, I liked being in the marines."

> ## "I'M NOT SURE THAT ACTING IS SOMETHING FOR A GROWN MAN TO BE DOING."
> ### —STEVE MCQUEEN

CHAPTER TWO

FROM ACTING SCHOOL TO HOLLYWOOD

THE NEIGHBORHOOD PLAYHOUSE SCHOOL OF THE THEATRE

An acting student McQueen was dating thought he had potential and suggested he accompany her to observe a class at the Neighborhood Playhouse School of the Theatre in Manhattan. Sanford Meisner, the drama coach, always opened his class with the statement, "The foundation of acting is the reality of doing."

After observing some classes, McQueen asked to talk to Meisner about acting, which led to a one-on-one interview and acceptance into the class of seventy-two students.

Meisner was a teacher of method acting, a technique in which an actor aspires to complete emotional identification with a part. Based on the teachings of Konstantin Stanislavski that caught on in the United States in the 1930s, it had fallen by the wayside. Thanks to Meisner, Lee Strasberg, and others, it was experiencing a revival. Marlon Brando was the ultimate American method actor. For years, Meisner had been searching for the next Brando, and in young McQueen, he thought he had found him.

Meisner said, "He was an original—both tough and childlike like Marilyn Monroe [another method actor], as if he'd been through everything but had preserved a certain basic innocence. I accepted him at once."

> "I'M FROM THE ACTORS STUDIO BUT AS FAR AS ANY SET METHOD IS CONCERNED, I DON'T BELIEVE THERE IS ONE. . . . AND I CERTAINLY ADMIRE MR. BRANDO, BUT I WOULDN'T WANT TO BE LIKE HIM."
>
> —STEVE MCQUEEN

SANFORD MEISNER

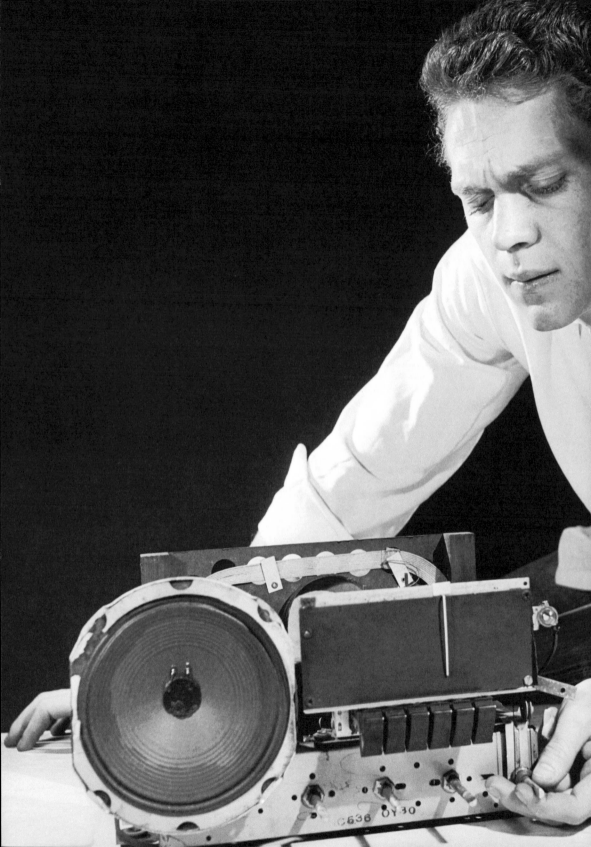

ACTORS STUDIO

In the 1950s, Lee Strasberg's Actors Studio, was considered method acting's Valhalla. When McQueen was accepted, he joined an acting pantheon that included Marilyn Monroe, James Dean, Paul Newman, Eli Wallach, and others.

McQueen auditioned for the studio in 1955 and performed a then-popular park scene monologue taken from Clifford Odets's *Golden Boy* about a young violinist who wants to be a prizefighter. It was a performance that impressed the demanding Strasberg. McQueen was one of only two actors accepted that year.

The typical Actors Studio role was that of the antihero, a role for which McQueen needed little coaching. Wallach, who was a student with McQueen at Actors Studio and would costar with him in *The Magnificent Seven* and *The Hunter*, recalled, "Even then, McQueen had the raw skill. His greatest talent lay in being observant. He could always find what in an earlier scene had led logically to what he was doing just then. . . . Nobody quite grasped the poetry in the flow of film like he did. What McQueen had learned to do was what separates the true artist from the ham—to watch and, above all, to listen. McQueen was the best reactor of his generation."

DENISE MCCLUGGAGE

"Steve was at a nowhere place in his career," recalled journalist, photographer, and race car driver Denise McCluggage about meeting McQueen in New York City in 1955 or 1956. She was a sports reporter for the *New York Herald Tribune*, and he was an aspiring actor. What they had in common was a car: the MG-TC. His was cream colored and hers was red. He was parked in front of a popular hangout in Greenwich Village, showing off his new MG-TC to friends, stating it was a gift from some English friends. She hung back, listening.

She later wrote that she "was touched by his almost waif-like quality—his delight and genuine surprise that someone would go to all the trouble to send him a present, particularly one he really dug. There was this incongruity in Steve's vulnerability, his cock-of-the-walk posturing, his jive talk. And if there's anything I'm a sucker for, it's incongruity." She mentioned that she was the owner of the red MG-TC he had seen. A beautiful woman who shared a love of cars *and* who had one like his . . . the conversation continued in the hangout and later in her five-flight walk-up around the corner. She

said they soon became a 'Village 'item.'" The demands of their careers caused them to soon part ways, he for Hollywood and she to start her career as a race car driver.

In 1962, they literally crossed paths, competing at Sebring, he driving an MGA for British Motor Corporation and she an O.S.C.A. Years later, as he was about to begin work on *Le Mans*, she learned he was in London as well and decided to try to see him at his hotel. By now he was a big star, and she was unsure if the bodyguard would believe her when she gave him her name, saying she was an old friend. A few minutes later she heard a voice call out, "Denise McCluggage. Now that's a name from the past!"

Upon hearing of his death over the car radio in 1980, she wrote that an image of him immediately came to mind: "I saw then that 1950s day in New York, and a young man with short-cropped hair wearing chino pants and a stark white T-shirt lounging against a cream-colored MG-TC with a machine-turned dashboard. He squints into the stark white sun and smiles a quick, not-yet-famous smile suddenly there, just as suddenly gone."

THE SALAD YEARS
EARLY MOVIES

SOMEBODY UP THERE LIKES ME

28

Director Robert Wise had his star for the movie *Somebody Up There Likes Me*: Paul Newman, a rising talent desperate to erase the memory of his role in the career-threatening debacle *The Silver Chalice*. Now Wise needed to round out his cast. *Somebody Up There Likes Me* told the story of middleweight boxing champion and legend Rocky Graziano. The boxer's early years were ugly, full of pain and punishment, fertile ground for an angry young man rebelling against all authority. It was a life rescued and given purpose in the boxing ring.

For the supporting cast in Graziano's early street-gang years, Wise needed actors with a chip-on-their-shoulder intensity, ruggedness, and vulnerability. It was thanks to his new wife Neile, who had a role as a dancer in Wise's previous movie *This Could be the Night*, that McQueen got entrée for what was a walk-on role. Wise recalled, "He came in, in a sport jacket, kind of gangly and loose and he had a little cap. . . . I guess it was his cocky manner somehow, not fresh, but just nice and cocky and a bit full of himself that just caught my eye and I cast him in this small part. It was the part of some kid on a rooftop fighting back in New York." The role was that of Fido, a gang member. McQueen was paid $19 a day.

When he wasn't acting, he was watching Newman, who was performing in what would prove to be his breakthrough role as Graziano. Not surprisingly, given the similarity of his early years with those of Graziano, McQueen felt that the lead role was something he should have had instead of Newman. What McQueen also saw in Newman was an actor getting the full-on star treatment, and he wanted it. From that point on, Newman became McQueen's career measuring stick.

> ## "IF YOU BLINKED TWICE IN THAT ONE YOU MISSED ME. BUT AT LEAST I'D NOTCHED A FEATURE CREDIT, WHICH GAVE ME A TOE IN THE DOOR."
>
> —STEVE MCQUEEN

THE BLOB

The Blob was a low-budget B-movie horror mashup of two movie trends in the 1950s: teenage rebellion and metaphorical paranoia (best described as "the commies are out to kill us," "science has run amok, creating giant insects or worse that are out to kill us," or "evil outer space aliens are out to kill us," and occasionally any combination thereof). The primary audience was the teenage drive-in movie crowd, though an occasional film like *Invasion of the Body Snatchers* would break out as a sleeper hit.

Needing money and believing the movie would bomb, McQueen opted for a flat-rate fee of $3,000 instead of 10 percent of the gross to star as teenager Steve Andrews (McQueen was then twenty-eight years old). As he later said, "The main acting challenge in this one consisted of running around, bug-eyed, and shouting, 'Hey, everybody, look out for the Blob!'"

The story is simple and straightforward: an amoeba-like alien life form is carried to Earth inside a meteorite and creates mayhem once free, and McQueen has to figure out a way to stop it before it consumes all life on Earth. On the surface, it seemed McQueen had made the right decision to accept a flat fee. After all, one critic called his antagonist "a lethal lump of interplanetary plum preserves." Another critic called *The Blob* "a crawling roomful of Jello that eats you instead of the other way around."

Teen audiences loved it, and the movie, budgeted at $240,000, made a whopping $12 million in its initial release. Had McQueen taken a percentage of the gross, he would have been a millionaire. Instead, that goal would have to wait.

> "I USUALLY PLAYED A KILLER OR A DELINQUENT, AND I DID A LOT OF SNARLING. . . . SO, I BEGAN LOOKING FOR SOMETHING TO IMPROVE MY IMAGE—AND WHAT I GOT WAS *THE BLOB*."
>
> —STEVE MCQUEEN

NEVER SO FEW

McQueen's role in the TV series *Wanted: Dead or Alive* had been paying the bills, but his goal was to be a successful movie star. Thanks to the way his contract was structured, McQueen was free to accept movie roles during the TV show's lull in production. In 1959, he landed the part of a wise-cracking supply sergeant in his first major production, *Never So Few*, a World War II drama starring Frank Sinatra as the leader of a guerilla band fighting Japanese troops in Burma.

When it came to their places in the Hollywood pecking order, McQueen and Sinatra were about as far apart as you could get, with McQueen at the base of Everest and Sinatra somewhere above its summit. Impressed and a little envious of the young actor's talent, Sinatra liked McQueen and displayed his affection in a series of pranks, usually involving exploding firecrackers around McQueen when he wasn't looking.

One time while McQueen was studying his lines, Sinatra snuck up and dropped a lit firecracker in McQueen's gun belt. The explosion caused McQueen to jump high in the air, much to Sinatra's delight.

McQueen decided that enough was enough and understood he had to stand up to the star or forever be the target of his pranks. McQueen later said, "So I grabbed one of the Tommy guns we were using in the film and jammed in a full clip—fifty rounds. Sinatra was walking away, laughing it up with his buddies, when I yelled at him, 'Hey, Frank!' He turned around and I let him have it, zap-zap-zap, the whole clip."

At close range, even the paper wadding from the blanks can hurt. Firing at full automatic, the submachine gun emptied in a few seconds. The stunned silence of the cast and crew seemed to last forever. McQueen said, "Everybody was watching Frank to see what he'd do. He had a real bad temper, and I guess they all figured we were gonna end in a punch-out. I wasn't sure myself, as we stared at each other. Then he just started laughing, and it was all over. After, we got along just fine."

Critics praised McQueen for his performance but savaged the movie. He didn't know it then, but with his next film, a Western, he'd strike movie gold.

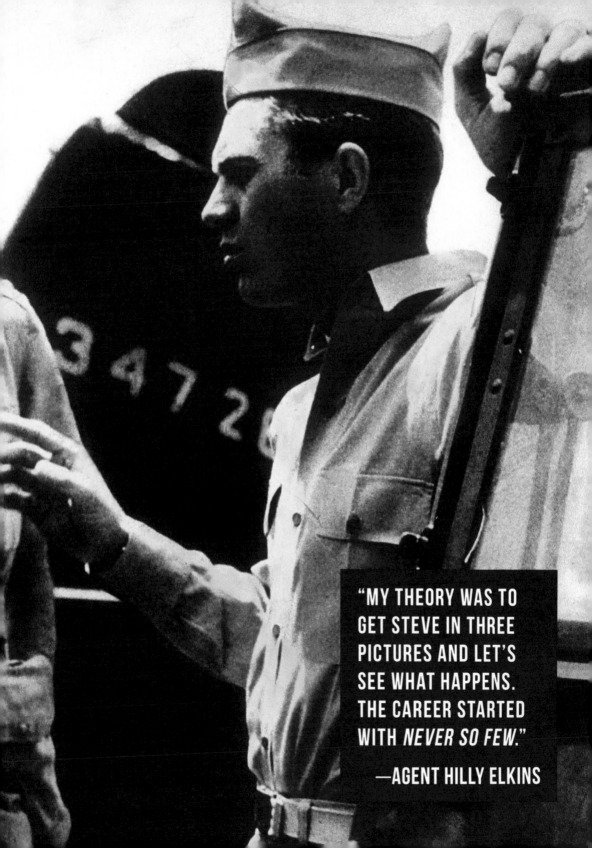

"MY THEORY WAS TO GET STEVE IN THREE PICTURES AND LET'S SEE WHAT HAPPENS. THE CAREER STARTED WITH *NEVER SO FEW*."

—AGENT HILLY ELKINS

CHAPTER FOUR

THE SALAD YEARS
TELEVISION

STUDIO ONE

Studio One, sometimes referred to as *Westinghouse Studio One* because Westinghouse was the program's sole sponsor, began as a radio anthology drama series that later moved to television. Immensely popular, it was one of the highest-rated shows during the Golden Age of Television in the 1950s. During its nine-year run on CBS, it received eighteen Emmy nominations, winning five. Among the many actors who began their careers in *Studio One* were Charlton Heston, Art Carney, Jack Lemon, and Leslie Nielsen.

In 1957, McQueen landed the role of a troubled youth accused of murder in "The Defender," a two-part episode. Ralph Bellamy and William Shatner play the father-son legal team representing McQueen. The episode was so well received that ratings significantly increased for the second part, and it was later spun off into its own series, *The Defenders*.

McQueen's performance was so strong that *Studio One* producer Herbert Brodkin sent him a personal letter on CBS stationery thanking him for helping make the show a hit. At the time, McQueen was dating dancer Neile Adams, whose career, unlike his, was both well-established and on an upward success curve. Hilly Elkins was one of Neile's agents. She had been begging Elkins to take on McQueen as a client. Elkins kept putting her off, because he thought that McQueen was a loser who was simply using Neile. Upon being told by her McQueen was appearing on *Studio One*, he agreed to watch the episode. After viewing the show, Elkins told her, "I saw one minute of 'The Defender' and he just broke through the screen." Elkins signed up McQueen.

> **"I SAW ONE MINUTE OF 'THE DEFENDER' AND HE JUST BROKE THROUGH THE SCREEN."**
>
> **—AGENT HILLY ELKINS**

WANTED: DEAD OR ALIVE

McQueen's breakthrough performance in "The Defender" was inspired by Neile. When he was struggling with how to play the part, she said, "Smile a little bit. I know it's a tough thing to do because you're playing a killer, but . . . you've got to be able to show something of you." He did, and suddenly the audience paid attention to him. McQueen would perfect that "smiley tough" persona as bounty hunter Josh Randall in the television Western series *Wanted: Dead or Alive*.

Originally, the story of Randall the bounty hunter appeared as an episode in the popular Western *Trackdown*. When he read the script, producer Vince Fennelly sensed that the Randall character could be spun off into his own series, provided he get the right actor.

Ironically, when he was offered it, McQueen originally rejected the part, claiming he didn't look the part of a Western hero. But Fennelly wanted anyone but the stereotypical tall good-guy hero. As he later explained, "A bounty hunter, by nature, is a sort of underdog. Everybody's against him—lawmen, bandits, townfolk. They don't like what he does for a living—hunting down fugitives and being paid a bounty for either capturing or killing them. So, if he's some big, aggressive football type

your audience will turn against him. I needed a kind of 'little guy' who looks tough enough to get the job done, but with a kind of boyish appeal behind the toughness. He had to be *vulnerable*, so the audience would root for him against the bad guys. McQueen was just what I had in mind. I knew he was my man the minute he walked through the door."

McQueen was convinced. He later said, "I liked Josh Randall. He was a lot like me—a loner who played his own games, made his own decisions. He was no hero strutting along with a badge pinned to his chest; he was a hired man doing a hired man's job for the money it paid him. I could identify with Randall, and I think the audience sensed that identification and responded to it."

Wanted: Dead or Alive debuted in September 1958. When it concluded three years later, McQueen was a bona fide television star. His agent, Elkins, said, "It had always been our plan that the road to film was through television, though at the time, no television star had ever made the transition from television to film." That was about to change.

FIREARMS

Westerns were huge in the 1950s. They were so popular that 1958 became known as the "Year of the Western." Seven of the top ten television programs were Westerns, with *Gunsmoke*, *Wagon Train*, *Have Gun Will Travel*, and *The Rifleman* taking the top four slots. In such a crowded field, McQueen knew he had to have something special to help make *Wanted: Dead or Alive* stand out. Because everyone else used Colt Peacemaker pistols or Winchester rifles, McQueen decided to do one better and carry something indelibly memorable.

McQueen worked with Kenny "Von Dutch" Howard to create what they called the "Mare's Leg" (a play on "hog leg," the slang term for revolver). He later said, "We took a Model 92 Winchester lever-action rifle and turned it into a belt gun by sawing off most of the barrel and fitting it with a special stock. This gave us the power and accuracy of a rifle with the mobility and easy handling of a revolver. And it *looked* fierce!"

It sure did! Toy manufacturers rushed to make cap gun versions, and they sold hand-over-fist to kids who wanted to look "Josh Randall

cool." Enthusiasm for the Mare's Leg continues, with several custom firearms manufacturers featuring Mare's Leg replicas in a variety of calibers. In 2014, one of the three known Mare's Legs made for the show was sold at auction in France for $23,700.

McQueen developed a passion for gun tricks and fast draws. During the filming of *Never So Few*, McQueen met and became friends with Sammy Davis Jr., who had the reputation of being the fastest quick-draw in Hollywood. Never one to resist a challenge, McQueen proposed a quick-draw-and-shoot contest. Davis accepted and a date was set, with the prize

"HE POSSESSES THAT COMBINATION OF SMOOTH-ROUGH CHARM THAT SUGGESTS STAR POSSIBILITIES"

—PAUL BECKLEY, *NEW YORK HERALD TRIBUNE*

being a nickel-plated commemorative Colt .45 Peacemaker revolver.
In the days leading up to the event,
McQueen secretly began training. Davis's friends made side bets
with McQueen, figuring there was
no way he could beat Davis. When
the match was over, McQueen said,
"Well, I guess all that practice paid
off, 'cuz I walked away with the
Peacemaker." And all the side bets.

McQueen amassed quite a few firearms during his lifetime, from toys
to pistols, rifles, and shotguns. They
were auctioned in 2006, and highlights included a Winchester Model
1873 (made in 1879) that sold
for more than $20,000, a Parker
Brothers 20-gauge double-barreled
shotgun that sold for more than
$7,500, and a Buck Rogers toy pis-
tol with holster that went for more
than $1,300.

CHAPTER FIVE

SEIZING THE LIMELIGHT

THE MAGNIFICENT SEVEN

A remake of Akira Kurosawa's *Seven Samurai*, John Sturges's *The Magnificent Seven* is the story of seven Western gunslingers who rescue a beleaguered Mexican village from bandits. Sturges wanted McQueen as one of the seven in the role of Vin Tanner, a part that had only seven lines of dialogue. Sturges promised to make up for it by giving him "the camera"—focusing the camera on him as much as possible.

Though Yul Brynner was the star, McQueen had the street smarts, guts, and determination to do things both big and small to steal the movie out from under him. The first scene to be shot was the seven fording a stream. Brynner was in the lead, with the six following behind to fill out the landscape. That's when Steve made his first move: he took off his hat, leaned over, scooped some river water into it, and doused himself. That set the tone for a nonstop competition between the hot television actor (McQueen in *Wanted: Dead or Alive*) and the Academy Award–winning star (Brynner in *The King and I*, *The Ten Commandments*, and so on).

McQueen would do such screen-stealing stunts as shaking a shotgun shell before inserting it into his shotgun as Brynner drove a hearse down the street. McQueen knew how to fast draw and shoot; Brynner was uncomfortable around guns. McQueen knew how to ride; Brynner could barely stay on a horse. As McQueen later said, "I was in my element, he wasn't."

Former agent and longtime friend Hilly Elkins said, "Steve wasn't going to take any shit from the bald fellow [Brynner]. And the bald fellow wasn't going to take any shit from Steve."

In another scene, Brynner is giving a speech to the group and McQueen is standing behind him—McQueen begins flipping a coin, stealing the scene. Brynner found out, and in their next scene together, he took off his cowboy hat.

> ## "I WAS A TREAT TO HIM."
>
> **—STEVE MCQUEEN ON YUL BRYNNER**

He knew no stunts from McQueen could distract the audience from Brynner's jet-black outfit and shiny bald head.

But in McQueen, Brynner had met his match. When production on *The Magnificent Seven* began, Yul Brynner was the star. The movie opened on October 23, 1960, though Brynner had top billing, the star was Steve McQueen. As one reviewer put it, "If he can ever get sprung from television, McQueen's going to be a big star."

And at the end of March 1961, after 117 episodes, *Wanted: Dead or Alive* was canceled. McQueen was overjoyed. He acknowledged, "I'll always owe [Josh Randall] one for giving me a running start in this business. Right now, I've got a real chance to grab that brass ring, and, man, you better believe I'm ready to do some grabbin'."

...nt like seven hundred...

MAGNIFICENT SEVEN

THE MIRISCH COMPANY PRESENTS

Co-STARRING

...HER · ELI WALLACH · STEVE McQUEEN

Magnificent Seven

...ON · ROBERT VAUGHN

And Introducing
HORST BUCHHOLZ

...IAM ROBERTS Produced and Directed by JOHN STURGES · A MIRISCH-ALPHA PICTURE

...WALTER MIRISCH ... ELMER BERNSTEIN   UNITED

ROBERT VAUGHN

Robert Vaughn had just come off his Academy Award–nominated role in *The Young Philadelphians* when he was chosen by director John Sturges for the part of the suave, traumatized veteran and outlaw, Lee, in *The Magnificent Seven*. It was there that he first met McQueen and came to know his intensely competitive nature.

Yul Brynner was *the* star in *The Magnificent Seven*, with McQueen a distant second in the pecking order, something McQueen was determined to change.

Vaughn recalled, "The rivalry between McQueen and Brynner was clear from the start. Steve started knocking on my door around 6:30 a.m., an hour before we were due on set. Our conversations were always along the same lines." McQueen would complain that Brynner was wearing a too-fancy pearl handled pistol or was taller than he was—nothing about Brynner was beneath his notice, even if it was wrong. In one early-morning knock on the door, McQueen told Vaughn, "Did you see the size of Brynner's horse? It's goddamn gigantic." Vaughn replied, "Actually, Steve, I've got the biggest horse of the Seven." McQueen stared at him and said,

"I don't give a f*** about your horse. It's Brynner's horse I'm worried about."

Vaughn and McQueen became close friends. In 1964, Vaughn was among the guests invited to McQueen and Neile's first major Hollywood party. At one point he stood on the patio, taking in the view of the ocean, when McQueen joined him. Vaughn asked him,

> "I GET SUICIDAL WHEN I HAVE TO WATCH MY FILMS. WHEN I SEE MYSELF UP THERE, 24 FEET HIGH ON THAT SCREEN, I'M INTO A COLD SWEAT. EACH TIME I THINK, 'MAN, THIS THING'S GONNA BOMB AT THE BOX OFFICE!'"
>
> —STEVE MCQUEEN

"When you were in New York in the Fifties, living in a cold-water flat and courting Neile on your bike, did you ever think you'd end up this way?" McQueen replied, "What makes you think I'm going to end up this way now?" After learning of McQueen's death, Vaughn reflected, "I'll always miss his unique way of looking at life."

Vaughn later become a television star in the series *The Man from U.N.C.L.E.* During that show's final season, McQueen offered his friend the part of ambitious politician Walter Chalmers in *Bullitt*. Vaughn read the script and confessed that he found the story so confusing that he couldn't make any sense of it and turned him down. McQueen persisted, sending him revised drafts and increasing the salary Vaughn would receive—McQueen *really* wanted his friend in the movie. When the latest draft arrived, along with McQueen's biggest offer, a six-figure price tag, Vaughn told McQueen, "You know, the picture is starting to look better and better to me."

COWBOY HATS

When it comes to headgear attire, nothing is more distinctive or character defining than John Stetson's invention: the cowboy hat. For most of his movies, McQueen's Stetson was the Cattleman or its variation, the Cutter. In *Tom Horn*, he made a little nod to local history. Regional differences in cowboy hat crease styles were more pronounced in Horn's lifetime, a reflection that people weren't as mobile then as they are now. As *Tom Horn* was set in Wyoming, McQueen wore a high-crowned Stetson Gus with a Montana crease (or Montana slope), so named because it originated at a Montana ranch and was adopted by Montana cowboys. In *Wanted: Dead or Alive*, McQueen sported a flat-crowned Stetson Telescope Crease (a.k.a. Gambler's Hat), which he was wearing when his friend and drinking buddy John Sturges stopped by at the end of a day's shooting.

John Sturges had signed on as director of *The Magnificent Seven*. Yul Brynner had been cast as the leader of the seven gunslingers who save a Mexican village from bandits. Sturges needed to round up the other six. One of the six he wanted was McQueen.

Sitting in McQueen's *Wanted: Dead or Alive* dressing room and drinking beers, Sturges made his pitch, telling McQueen that he was doing an American version of Akira Kurosawa's *Seven Samurai*. "C'mon now, Johnny, I could never play a samurai," McQueen protested. "They'd hoot me off the screen."

Sturges smiled. "You've got it wrong. I'm not doing a remake. I'm taking the basic plot and doing it as an American Western."

"Well . . ." McQueen replied dubiously.

Sturges leaned forward and flicked his finger on the brim of McQueen's sweat-stained Stetson and said, "Hell, you won't even have to change your hat!"

McQueen did, in fact, change his cowboy hat. Vin Tanner's wearing a Stetson Cattleman. And McQueen would use it as a scene-stealing prop as much as possible during the movie, most notably in an early scene when the gunslingers are crossing a stream. Brynner is in the lead. McQueen is riding directly behind him. From cowboy hat to boots, Brynner attire is black—the

dience's eye. Shortly after they begin to ford the stream, McQueen takes off his hat, leans over and scoops up a hatful of water and places it back on his head. Co-star and friend Robert Vaughn recalled, "Water cascaded down on [McQueen's] head and shoulders, soaking him thoroughly. He looked like a fool, but at least no one was looking at Yul Brynner."

McQueen's first cowboy hat was made by Eddy Baron, "Hollywood's Hat Maker," of Baron's Hats. Founded during Hollywood's golden age, Baron's ledger in which he recorded the size of each client's head contains a who's-who list of Hollywood greats.

Sometimes the actor would come to Baron's store in Burbank for the fitting. But it was not uncommon, as in the case of John Wayne and other big stars, for Baron to go to the actor's home. A few years ago, Baron Hats issued a special edition of McQueen's Josh Randall hat. Named "The Bounty Hunter," production was limited to one hundred hats. If you were lucky to buy one and your hat size is 7 inches, you'd be doubly blessed with the McQueen look: that was the King of Cool's hat size.

HELL IS FOR HEROES

The title could be applied to the making of this grim World War II drama as well. McQueen's success in *The Magnificent Seven* was followed by embarrassing failure in *The Honeymoon Machine*. Angry over that and the fact that he missed out on getting the role he wanted in *Pocketful of Miracles* and looking to get his career back on track, he thought he found the right vehicle with *Separation Hill*. The problem was he didn't like the script's title, thought his role as Private John Reese was too small, hated the director, didn't get along with the cast, and despised the penny-pinching studio executives who underbudgeted the film and repeatedly threatened to stop production. Other than that, it was perfect.

Set in Germany in 1944, it's the story of a ragtag collection of seven GIs ordered to hold their position against a vastly superior enemy. Through guise, guile, and desperate heroics, all the while overcoming clashes among themselves, the soldiers manage to hold off the German troops, but at great cost to themselves. The film ends with Reese heroically eliminating a German pillbox at the cost of his life.

McQueen got the name changed to *Hell Is for Heroes*, his role expanded, and a new director in Academy Award–winner Don Siegel, and he stood up to the executives. As it turned out, the behind-the-scenes drama and tensions worked to the movie's benefit. Though a modest box office success, *Hell Is for Heroes* was recognized by critics then and film historians later as a low-budget antiwar masterpiece.

Hell Is for Heroes became a cult favorite and one of the most requested of his movies in McQueen film festivals. Its impact extended to television decades later in the science-fiction series *Deep Space Nine* in an episode called "The Siege of AR-558," which was inspired by the movie.

Shortly after its release, McQueen received a congratulatory telegram from an up-and-coming director who wrote, "Dear Steve, I want to congratulate you for your performance in *Hell Is for Heroes*. It's the most perceptive and realistic performance of any soldier in any war film I have seen. Best regards, Stanley Kubrick."

THE WAR LOVER

Frustration can either breed more frustration or be the catalyst for opportunity. For McQueen, it proved the latter. Deciding he needed a change in scenery in the wake of the *Hell Is for Heroes* disappointment, McQueen signed on to do *The War Lover*. Another World War II drama, it had one thing going for it that McQueen couldn't resist: though produced by Columbia, it would be shot on location in England. There, he'd be neighbors with Formula One racing legend, and his friend, Stirling Moss. To the studio's great displeasure (it forced McQueen to sign an agreement to pay it $2.5 million if he had an accident that halted production), McQueen whiled away his off hours with Moss and racing.

An accident while racing at Brands Hatch in his Cooper that almost killed him wound up helping the film. In the movie's final moments, a wounded Rickson keeps his badly damaged B-17 aloft long enough for the rest of the crew to parachute out before it crashes into a cliff, killing him. McQueen's minor facial wounds added to the realism of that climactic scene.

McQueen's role in *The War Lover* in many respects resembled that of his role in *Hell Is for Heroes* with two exceptions: B-17 pilot Captain Buzz Rickson had a higher rank and a worse personality. Enamored with battle, arrogant, callous with his squadron mates' lives, and seeing women only as sexual objects to be violently conquered, Rickson was McQueen's most challenging role to date. Of Rickson, McQueen said, "He's selfish and selfless. He

> "HE REVELS IN WAR AND DESTRUCTION. HE LIVES FOR KILLING. I'VE GOT TOO INVOLVED WITH HIM. BY THE TIME I GET HOME AT NIGHT, AFTER A DAY'S WORK, I'M PHYSICALLY AND MENTALLY EXHAUSTED."
>
> —STEVE MCQUEEN

has the respect of a crew that pretty generally hates him. But Rickson is one hell of a flyer . . . can make a B-17 stand on its tail and dance. His love of war makes him incapable of love for other human beings." Released four months after *Hell Is for Heroes*, it was a critical and commercial failure. Deeply disappointed, McQueen devoted himself to racing, where he wound up achieving success on the track that kept eluding him on the big screen. Following his winning of several races, he received an offer from John Cooper and British Motor Corporation to race in Europe. McQueen later confessed, "I didn't know if I was an actor who raced or a racer who acted." With a wife and two young children to support, McQueen turned down the offer and decided to devote himself to acting. It was good that he did, for a brighter future was about to unfold.

THE GREAT ESCAPE

Director John Sturges told McQueen, "The loner's the part you want." The "part" was that of American Captain Virgil Hilts, "the Cooler King," so named because of the punishment he received in the cooler—a solitary confinement cell—for his many failed attempts to escape from German prisoner of war camps. The movie was *The Great Escape*, a drama based on the largest Allied prisoner-of-war escape attempt during World War II.

Like *The Magnificent Seven*, this was another Sturges "team" story. Though McQueen would have top billing, unlike *Seven* where Brynner had the main role, *Escape* was originally an ensemble movie with no real leading role. And, as originally written, the role of Hilts was so spare and ill defined as to almost be a cameo. When McQueen saw a rough cut of the first six weeks of shooting and the contrast between his bare-bones character and that of the others, particularly James Garner's "Scrounger," he walked out, stating that his role had to be rewritten and expanded. The crisis escalated, threatening to shut down production.

Meetings between star, director, and co-stars ensued. Ideas were thrashed out. With the acceptance of McQueen's demands, the tone of the movie changed—and movie history was made.

McQueen insisted Hilts's number of solo escape attempts be increased. That loner aspect and his baseball-and-glove routine became a motif throughout the movie. But McQueen's greatest contribution, one that came to define the movie, was at the climax, a scene he had insisted on from the beginning: a motorcycle jump scene.

Though McQueen did most of his motorcycle riding in the movie,

> "WHEN I DID *THE GREAT ESCAPE*, I KEPT THINKING, 'IF THEY WERE MAKING A MOVIE OF MY LIFE, THAT'S WHAT THEY'D CALL IT—THE GREAT ESCAPE."
>
> —STEVE MCQUEEN

friend and fellow biker Bud Ekins performed the stunt for insurance reasons. His motorcycle was a Triumph TR6 Trophy, one of four used in the movie, customized by Von Dutch (very imperfectly, given the different engine configurations) to look like a BMW R75 German army motorcycle. A ramp was constructed in a wallow to increase the angle for the jump.

With McQueen watching behind the camera, second unit director Robert Relyea shouted, "Action!" Ekins dropped his clutch, gunned the Triumph's throttle, roared down into the wallow and up the ramp, and flew an arching sixty feet through the air and over a six-foot-high wood-and barbed-wire fence. One of the most vivid and breathtaking scenes in movie history was accomplished in one take.

Released in the summer of 1963, *The Great Escape* was an international smash hit, with audiences going wild over the jump scene. Now the hottest name in Hollywood, McQueen became the first actor to successfully make the professional leap from television celebrity to international movie star.

THE GREAT ESCAPE MOTORCYCLE

The motorcycle McQueen (okay, okay, Bud Ekins) rode in the iconic climactic jump scene in *The Great Escape* technically should have been a BMW R75, the model used by the German army in World War II, or a postwar BMW modified to resemble one. But, as McQueen explained to biographer and friend William Nolan, "We couldn't use a real BMW, not at the speed we were running, since those old babies were rigid-frame jobs and couldn't take the punishment." Instead, McQueen and Ekins tapped a bike they knew intimately and loved: the 650cc Triumph TR6 Trophy.

Bud Ekins owned one of the first Triumph motorcycle dealerships in the United States. An accomplished businessman as well as an award-winning hare-and-hound rider, he was instrumen-

> ## "STEVE ALWAYS GAVE ME CREDIT FOR THE JUMP."
>
> —BUD EKINS

tal in getting Triumph to produce bigger-engined bikes to go head-to-head with big-bored Harley-Davidsons in the American market (previously Triumph's largest bike was the 500cc TR5 Trophy). With high-end power (for the time) of 42 bhp and speed (a true 100 miles per hour), McQueen and Ekins knew the TR6 could deliver what was needed: a dramatic off-road jump over a six-foot barbed wire fence.

Vehicle customizer Von Dutch's modifications of the Triumphs used in the film were largely cosmetic: a military paint scheme and headlight, a rear luggage rack, and some other superficial touches. The most significant structural change was with the suspension to make it sturdy enough to handle the stresses of the jump.

The Australian motocross champion Tim Gibbes was part of the movie's stunt-riding crew. After conferring with the special effects manager, Ekins and Gibbes went to the natural wallow near where the six-foot Swiss-German border fence had been set up to work out details. An initial test run revealed that, in order to clear the fence, they needed to modify the slope,

creating a spoon-shaped ramp. After several test runs and more digging of the wallow, Ekins was able to reach 60 miles per hour in fourth gear, leap twelve feet into the air, and travel sixty-five feet.

On the day of the shoot, Ekins said, "I backed the Triumph off and then got on it hard. When I took off, I throttled right back and it was silent. You know, everything was just silent—the whole crew and everything was just silent and then when I landed they were cheering like crazy." One of the most famous stunt scenes in movie history was completed in just one take.

In 2012, Triumph issued a special T100 Steve McQueen Edition Limited to 1,100 individually numbered bikes. It was patterned to replicate the Triumph used in the movie and carried reproductions of McQueen's signature on the side panels.

JAMES COBURN

James Coburn got to know McQueen through a number of guest appearances in *Wanted: Dead or Alive*, and they quickly became close friends. Their next professional linkup was in the movie *Hell Is for Heroes*. Coburn recalled that they were on location near Redding, California, where temperatures got up to 110 degrees Fahrenheit in the shade, forcing production to shoot at night. Coburn said the studio gave McQueen a convertible to use in his downtime. "And we'd be driving along the road," Coburn said, "and all of the sudden he'd shoot off the road and go tearing through the woods, as fast as he could until he ran into something! So he wore this car out in about a week and a half, and they sent a guy out who said, 'What the hell happened to this car?!' Steve said, 'I dunno. It just stopped running.'" McQueen wound up crashing three rental cars, causing Coburn to finally quit riding with him.

Coburn would work with McQueen in two more films, *The Magnificent Seven* and *The Great Escape*. Following McQueen's death, Coburn said of his longtime friend, "As for his life, it was like he bought a Harley-Davidson and rode it until it came to pieces. He squeezed everything into his life. He shouldn't have been sad for a minute of it, because he got everything out of it that was possible."

LOVE WITH THE PROPER STRANGER

White hot in the box office and with the male audience firmly in the palm of his hand following the release of *The Great Escape*, McQueen's next roll would cement his appeal with the female audience. In *Love with the Proper Stranger*, McQueen played bed-'em-and-leave-'em loser trumpeter Rocky Papasano. It was McQueen's first romantic lead role. More importantly, the part of Papasano had first been offered to Paul Newman, who turned it down. McQueen saw it as his opportunity to outdo Newman.

A social consciousness film that confronted the issue of abortion (which was illegal until *Roe v. Wade* in 1973), it's the story of a one-night stand between Papasano and Angela Rossini (Natalie Wood) and their up-and-down relationship following Rossini's revelation that she's pregnant and considering having an abortion. Shocked by conditions in the illegal abortion clinic, ne'er-do-well Papasano has a crisis of conscience and decides he can't let Rossini get the abortion. The movie ends with them deciding to marry, a budding love having replaced lust.

Set and largely shot in New York City, McQueen had both the real-life and acting New York City "street cred" needed for the role—something Newman didn't have. In his performance, McQueen displayed a combination of vulnerability, humor, gentleness, and controlled masculine sexuality that captivated female audiences. *The Great Escape* made McQueen an international action hero; *Love with the Proper Stranger* made him an international sex symbol.

> "IT SHOWED ALL THE ASPECTS THAT MADE HIM REALLY APPEAL TO WOMEN SO MUCH, BECAUSE IT SHOWED THIS MACHO MAN WHO DARED TO BE VULNERABLE."
>
> —NEILE ADAMS MCQUEEN

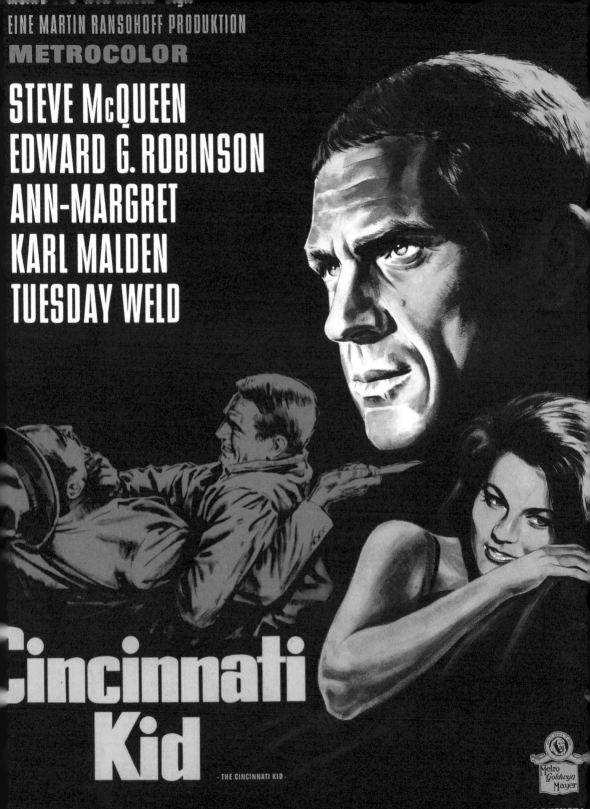

EINE MARTIN RANSOHOFF PRODUKTION
METROCOLOR

STEVE McQUEEN
EDWARD G. ROBINSON
ANN-MARGRET
KARL MALDEN
TUESDAY WELD

Cincinnati
Kid

· THE CINCINNATI KID ·

...AN BLONDELL · RIP TORN · JACK WESTON · CAB CALLOWAY · Drehbuch: RING LARDNER jr. und TERRY SOUTHERN
...ch einem Roman von Richard Jessup · Regie: Norman Jewison · Ein Filmways Solar Film

THE CINCINNATI KID

After a one-year hiatus from moviemaking, McQueen signed on for the title role in *The Cincinnati Kid*. Set for the most part in Depression-era New Orleans, it's the story of Eric "the Kid" Stoner, a brash, up-and-coming poker player out to prove he's the best. His quest culminates in a dramatic high-stakes poker game with "the Man," Lancey Howard, the acknowledged poker king, played by Edward G. Robinson.

In many respects, the movie had a real-life counterpart thanks to the casting of young star McQueen and seasoned veteran Robinson. It was a situation Robinson acknowledged: "Once, back at the start of my career, I had *been* another McQueen. I'd played the same kind of parts, cocky and tough, ready to take on the old timers and beat them at their own game. I identified strongly with McQueen, and I had a lot of respect for his talent."

Despite McQueen feeling that the movie would "bomb at the box office," *The Cincinnati Kid* was a smash hit both domestically and internationally—the first of five back-to-back hits for McQueen. The movie has since been acknowledged as the definitive film on poker, with McQueen's performance as one of the best in his career. With *The Cincinnati Kid*, McQueen began a ten-year run of making the list of top ten favorite box office stars.

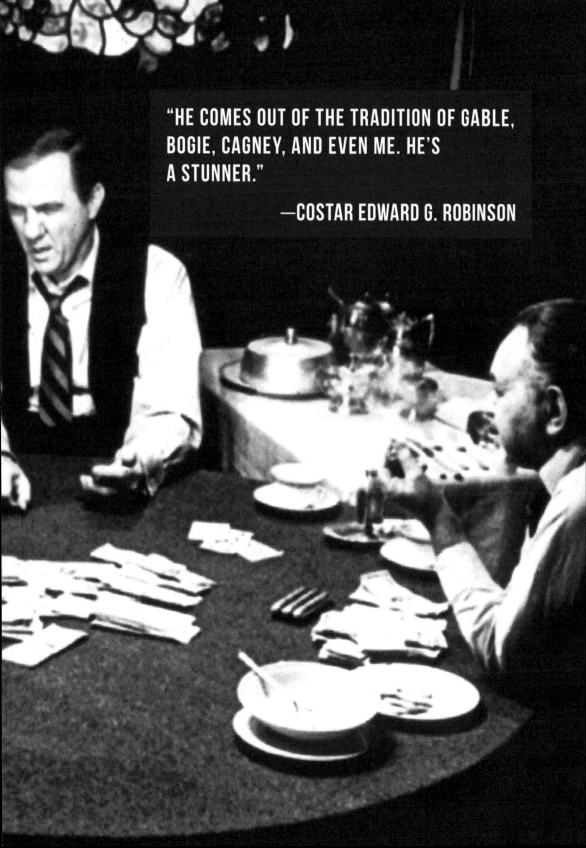

"HE COMES OUT OF THE TRADITION OF GABLE, BOGIE, CAGNEY, AND EVEN ME. HE'S A STUNNER."

—COSTAR EDWARD G. ROBINSON

NEVADA SMITH

After *The Cincinnati Kid*, McQueen returned to the Westerns with *Nevada Smith*, the story of a half-white, half-Kiowa Max Sand— "Nevada Smith"—and his quest to avenge the brutal murder of his parents by outlaws.

Veteran Western director Henry Hathaway was inked for the project. Aware of McQueen's confrontational reputation with directors, Hathaway laid down the law with McQueen in their first meeting, stating, "If you've got some ideas, I'll listen. But don't you get bullheaded and scream and holler at me, because I'll holler and scream back. I'm the meanest son-of-a-bitch that ever was!" After a moment's silence, McQueen smiled, offered his hand, and said, "All right, Mr. Hathaway. You've got a deal."

What followed was a getting-to-know-each-other meeting. Near its end, McQueen said, "I've got a guy who doubles me, and he's going to double me on this film." Hathaway firmly replied, "That's nice, but I have my favorite stuntman, and he doubles my leads in all my movies." An argument erupted, with Hathaway finally stating, "Listen, you little son-of-a-bitch, nobody's doubling you but Loren and that's that!" When McQueen asked who he meant, Hathaway shouted, "Loren Janes. That's who's going to double you!" McQueen replied, "That's who I'm talking about!" The two men then roared with laughter and had a smooth relationship during the shoot.

Nevada Smith was McQueen's second worldwide smash and confirmed him as the biggest international star of the day. Studio heads, wanting to exploit the early stages of a rocketing career, made offers of up to 50 percent of the gross if he would sign a contract.

> "HE'S NOT AFRAID TO USE HIMSELF WHEN HE ACTS. STEVE HAS WHAT I CALL A KIND OF DARING THEATRICALITY."
>
> —DIRECTOR ROBERT MULLIGAN

THE SAND PEBBLES

McQueen's name had come up for the lead role of Jake Holman in *The Sand Pebbles* as early as 1963, but, director Robert Wise wanted Paul Newman, a bigger star. (*The Great Escape* had not yet been released.) When Newman dropped out, McQueen's star power was concurrently hitting its peak, so McQueen became a shoo-in for the lead role. *The Sand Pebbles* is the story of Holman, an independent, insubordinate US Navy machinist mate first class who gets along better with the gunboat *San Pablo*'s engine than he does with the crew and the *San Pablo*'s efforts to rescue American missionaries trapped in civil-war-torn China in the 1920s.

Wise, who had given McQueen his walk-on role in *Somebody Up There Likes Me* in 1956, marveled at how high McQueen had since risen. Shooting on location in Taiwan, Wise later said, "I never dreamed I'd be working with him here in the Orient as the star of a multi-million-dollar production. But the truth is, he's a perfect choice for the part of Jake Holman. I've never seen an actor work with mechanical things the way he does. He learned everything about operating that ship's engine, just as Holman did in the script. Jake Holman is a very strong individual who doesn't bend under pressure, a guy desperately determined to maintain his own personal identity and pride. Very much like Steve."

Location shooting was done in Taiwan and Hong Kong and was plagued by problems that included everything from real-life political

> "I THINK THAT HE WAS UNIQUE IN THE FACT THAT HE CHOSE TO DO LESS ON THE SCREEN. BY DOING LESS, HE BROUGHT SIMPLICITY ON THE SCREEN, AND AT THE SAME TIME HE WAS VERY MUCH THE IMAGE OF THE AMERICAN MAN."
>
> —COSTAR MAKO

turmoil to monsoons. The scheduled two months became a grueling marathon of seven months that left the cast and crew exhausted.

It was worth it. Unlike previous roles where McQueen had to invent or add to the character, the Holman role proved to be a rich feast from the get-go. McQueen bit into it so deeply that, as the ancient belief states, he "ate the cow and inhaled its soul." As biographer Marc Eliot wrote, in Holman, McQueen found his on-screen signature, "a powerful, attractive, strong, unsmiling antihero." Prior to *The Sand Pebbles*, Hollywood called the shots in defining the identity of a Steve McQueen hero. After *The Sand Pebbles*, the roles were reversed, with McQueen defining what a Hollywood hero was.

Released in 1966, in addition to being another domestic and international hit, *The Sand Pebbles* was nominated for eight Academy Awards, with McQueen getting his first, and as it turned out, only, Oscar nomination for Best Actor.

THE THOMAS CROWN AFFAIR

Neile Adams McQueen was McQueen's most important advisor when it came to accepting movie roles. After he recovered from *The Sand Pebbles*, an experience that included a difficult-to-shake bout of flu and an abscessed molar, Neile handed him a script she said would be the perfect follow up. It was a radical, 180-degree turn away from the moody, misanthropic Holman. This movie's character was urbane, sophisticated, fashionable James Bond type. The part was going to be a real challenge, but she was dead certain audiences, especially women, would love him. It was an offbeat caper movie full of twists and turns whose central character, a wealthy self-made man, relieves boredom by executing the perfect robbery and is stalked by a beautiful insurance investigator (Faye Dunaway) determined to see him behind bars.

Shot in and around Boston, *The Thomas Crown Affair* is rich with Boston Brahmin elegance and atmosphere. Though there are many memorable scenes in the movie, three stand out. One is the erotic "love game" chess match between McQueen and Dunaway that was copied, move for move, from a match played by chess masters Gustav Zeissl and Walter von Walthoffen in Vienna in 1899.

Another scene was the polo match, for which McQueen had to learn how to play polo. Prior to *Thomas Crown*, his experience riding horses was on a Western saddle. As he quickly discovered, polo ponies and the English saddle were different. McQueen later said, "The first time the horse stopped quick I was right up on his neck hanging onto his ears. He was a lot smarter than I was. He knew the game and I

> "THERE'S A FEELING OF CONTROL IN HIM THAT A WOMAN RESPONDS TO. . . . HE STIMULATES THAT CUDDLY FEELING. HE'S THE MISUNDERSTOOD BAD BOY YOU'RE SURE YOU CAN CURE WITH A LITTLE WARMTH AND SOME HOME COOKING."
>
> —COSTAR FAYE DUNAWAY

didn't. He'd go left—and I'd go right, flat on my butt. A polo pony is guided by knee pressure, leaving your arms free to swing the mallet. I finally got the hang of it and began having fun batting down that field."

A third scene involved, of course, a vehicle. In this case, it was a dune buggy that McQueen helped customize. When not involved in shooting, McQueen would take it out for joy rides along the beach, much to director Norman Jewison's frustration when McQueen failed to show up for scenes.

One scene with the dune buggy almost ended in disaster. Jewison wanted McQueen, with Dunaway as passenger, to do a high-speed race to the surf and then, at its edge, horse the dune buggy around, sending out a dramatic high arc of spray. But when the moment came to turn the wheel, McQueen said, "The thing just wouldn't turn. Then the throttle jammed—and we were heading right for the ocean at a terrific rate of speed." The dune buggy plunged into the water, and the two emerged soaked but unharmed.

As Neile predicted, women loved McQueen as the devilishly suave Crown. The Belles of Memphis, a group of Southern college women, voted McQueen "the sexiest man in America."

THE THOMAS CROWN AFFAIR
DUNE BUGGY

Picture this: In *The Thomas Crown Affair*, Vicki Anderson gets behind the wheel of her Jeep and takes Thomas Crown out for a spin on the beach. That's how the beach scene was originally written, but that idea flew out the car window faster than a flicked cigarette once McQueen signed on. Vicki went from driver to passenger and the Jeep became a "Queen Manx"—a souped-up Meyers Manx dune buggy.

In the 1960s, a Meyers Manx dune buggy was a kit car whose essential feature was a cool-looking molded fiberglass body bolted onto a VW Beetle chassis. But McQueen wanted a dune buggy with more oomph than what could be coaxed from a stock, air-cooled VW four-banger. He partnered with Con-Ferr Manufacturing in Burbank, California, to design the Queen Manx. Of his work on the design, McQueen later said, "I'm rather proud of that."

The conversion was extensive but was completed in just eight weeks. Power was supplied by a 140-horsepower Corvair engine fed by a four-barrel carburetor. Jon Harting worked for Con-Ferr at the time and was part of the team that built the Queen Manx. After being told by owner Pete Condos to go to work on the dune buggy, Harting said, "I bought the Corvair engine from a wrecking yard and brought it back to the shop and steam-cleaned it. We attached it to a VW transaxle that was in a VW chassis. The body was all hand-laid fiberglass and custom built in our shop. I remember Steve coming by to look at its progress on two occasions. Both times he drove a red Maserati roadster. He was real nice to all of us there."

McQueen had a ball racing the high-powered dune buggy on

> "WE DID ONE BIG JUMP FOR THE CAMERA RIGHT OFF THE EDGE OF A HIGH DUNE AND IT WAS WILD."
>
> —STEVE MCQUEEN

the beach and over the dunes. He later said that Faye Dunaway deserved a Purple Heart for riding with him—the dramatic moment when the dune buggy plows into the surf happened by accident. Originally, McQueen was supposed to barrel straight toward the water and then, at the last second, horse the dune buggy around right at the water's edge. But, the moment he was supposed to turn the vehicle, McQueen said nothing happened. "The thing just wouldn't turn," he recalled. "Then the throttle jammed—and we were heading right for the ocean at a terrific rate of speed. Well, on film, all you could see was this orange bug disappearing into the water. Faye came out of it soaked and smiling. Some trooper! They had to take the whole engine apart to get the salt water out."

Thanks to its appearance in the movie, Manx mania swept the nation and sales of Meyers Manx dune buggies and unauthorized knockoffs skyrocketed.

SUITS IN THE THOMAS CROWN AFFAIR

The phrase "the clothes make the man" was truly the case for McQueen in *The Thomas Crown Affair*. McQueen's persona both on and off screen was the antithesis of the elegant, three-piece-suit-and-tie-wearing Thomas Crown. And that extreme difference and contrast in background and lifestyle caused McQueen to struggle to get inside Crown's skin.

The solution, as it turned out, was to put Crown's skin—his suits—on McQueen. The moment he donned his suits (designed by the Savile Row "tailor to the stars" Douglas Hayward), McQueen not only looked the part—he *became* Thomas Crown.

McQueen is first seen in a classic British single-breasted three-piece suit, medium gray with a muted Glen Plaid or "Prince of Wales" check that contains hints of blue. It is complimented by a powder-blue silk shirt with French cuffs and mother-of-pearl cufflinks, along with a French blue silk tie. In his waistcoat is a gold hunter-cased Patek Philippe pocket watch, worn on a thick double Albert chain with a Phi Beta Kappa key fob. *Trés chic*!

Equally famous was his less formal attire. For example, the navy nylon windbreaker, khakis slacks, Persols, and tan suede chukka boots that he wore in the glider scene were quintessentially McQueen: a sporty outfit that was more than casual— it was cool casual.

Cary Grant biographer Richard Torregrossa and fashion designers Ralph Lauren and Tom Ford (the latter also an accomplished movie producer, director, and screenwriter) stated that *The Thomas Crown Affair* became one of the most influential events in defining what was men's style. McQueen's combination of confident masculinity and sense of classic menswear elegance in both formal and informal attire brilliantly sealed the movie's iconic position as a men's fashion arbiter.

PERSOL SUNGLASSES

When it comes to fashion, few things beat out sunglasses for being cool. And, in the world of sunglasses, nothing tops a pair of Persols, the epitome of Italian luxury eyewear. The Turin-based optical company was founded in 1917, originally making special eyewear for pilots and race car drivers. In 1962, Persol sunglasses became widely available in the US market, with McQueen becoming both an early purchaser and trendsetter. Since then, the list of Hollywood stars who have donned the iconic sunglasses has grown to include Greta Garbo, Paul Newman, Cary Grant, Daniel Craig, Ryan Gosling, and Leonardo DiCaprio.

Individually handcrafted, using the best hardware and most advanced premium glass lenses, the Persol design projects elegant style and luxury, automatically making anyone wearing a pair look cool.

McQueen ultimately accumulated a vast collection of Persols. His most famous pair was the 714, the first-ever folding sunglass model. For *The Thomas Crown Affair*, McQueen wore light Havana (tan) 714s with blue lenses customized for him. Persol later issued a special 714SM (for "Steve McQueen") model.

Persols are so identified with McQueen that in 2006, when a pair from his collection was put up for auction, it sold for $70,000.

BULLITT

Of all the character-defining movies in his career, *Bullitt* is widely regarded as *the* Steve McQueen movie. The irony is that at first Steve McQueen did not want to do *Bullitt*. His many brushes with the law as a youth had formed a negative attitude toward police. But after thinking about it, he changed his mind and was part of a film that forever changed action movies.

The movie's story is a complex tale of deceit and rough justice. In a pivotal moment, Lieutenant Frank Bullitt, a maverick in the San Francisco Police Department, is marked for death by the mob. Bullitt, in his Ford Mustang GT-390 Fastback, sees the hitman's Dodge Charger R/T 440 and turns the tables.

What happens next is a scene that riveted movie audiences to their seats: a ten-minute car chase thrill ride through the streets of San Francisco and beyond that not only defined the movie, but also became a benchmark by which all subsequent chase scenes were measured. Executive producer Robert Relyea said it "evolved out of McQueen's love for racing and the potential we all saw in San Francisco's rollercoaster streets to provide an unusual twist."

Released on October 17, 1968, it was a critical and box-office smash, winning an Academy Award (editing) and an Edgar Award (screenplay). In 2007, the Library of Congress selected it for preservation in its National Film Registry for being "culturally, historically, or aesthetically significant."

> "WITHOUT *BULLITT* THERE WOULD BE NO *THE FRENCH CONNECTION* . . . AND DON SIEGEL'S *DIRTY HARRY* OWES MORE THAN A LITTLE TO THE CHARACTER, STYLE, AND FEEL OF *BULLITT*."
>
> —MCQUEEN BIOGRAPHER MARC ELIOT

THE BULLITT
MUSTANG FASTBACK

Two factory-built 1968 Ford Mustang GT-390 Fastbacks were rolled into the shop of Hollywood car-builder and racer Max Balchowsky. What emerged weeks later were two customized muscle cars with dark Highland Green paint and jet-black grills, stripped of all exterior adornment, possessing the look and power they'd need to tear through the winding and hilly streets of San Francisco and across the nation at speeds of up to 110 miles per hour.

The year 1968 was arguably the height of the golden era of Detroit muscle cars. But despite competition from the menagerie of Chargers, Cougars, Road Runners, and Barracudas, as well as Trans Ams, GTOs, and more, *Bullitt*'s memorable Ford Mustang left them all in the dust.

In 2001, the Ford Motor Company rolled out a commemorative edition of the *Bullitt* Mustang. The response was so strong that it produced a commemorative fortieth anniversary edition in 2008. Such is the golden touch of the King of Cool.

THE BULLITT LOOK

McQueen wore many outfits in *Bullitt*. Of particular note was his navy-blue suit tailored by legendary British designer Douglas Hayward. Though it's dynamite, it's not fitting for the King of Cool here—a fact underscored when he discards it for what immediately became known as the "*Bullitt* Look," the outfit he wore in the immortal car chase scene and while riding with co-star Jacqueline Bisset in her yellow Porsche cabriolet: a brown herringbone tweed shooting jacket (how appropriate!), a dark blue

roll neck, charcoal slacks, and, of course, his signature brown suede desert boots. Aside from the fact that it's a good-looking ensemble, it's considered the *"Bullitt* Look" because it's the combination McQueen wore in the second half of the movie.

Created by Academy Award–winning costume designer Theadora Van Runkle, the jacket projects a look of casual sophistication, one both comfortable and elegant—and versatile in the case of Lieutenant Frank Bullitt! Then, when McQueen doffs it, he strips away the elegant veneer and reveals his magnetic virility, touched with menace, a look forever enshrined in the classic movie poster.

If ever there were a truly signature item in the McQueen ensemble that goes beyond that of movie prop (even though it made its appearance often enough in his films), it's his brown suede desert boots, which he wore both on and off screen. Also known as chukka boots, he was first seen wearing them in *The Blob*. He even managed to slip on a pair for *Papillon*.

In January 2014, the *Bullitt* jacket was sold in auction for $120,000.

PAPILLON

McQueen's next movie, *Papillon*, took him to hell on earth. *Papillon* (French for "butterfly") is the story of the indomitable will to be free regardless of the odds. Based on the international bestselling autobiography by Henri Charrière, it's the story of a safecracker framed for the murder of a pimp, sentenced to life in prison, and eventually incarcerated in France's notorious tropical Devil's Island in French Guiana, where he repeatedly attempted to escape, eventually succeeding in reaching Venezuela.

McQueen played Charrière, a role that would be his most complicated ever, but one in which he found much common ground. Comparing himself to Charrière, he later said, "I kept being driven by this restless feeling. I seemed always to be looking for something—never knowing what it was—but always there was the sense that I couldn't be confined. And that's exactly what I felt in common with Charrière's Papillon. This man, who had been restless and moving, suddenly found himself imprisoned, and his natural behavior and involuntary reaction was, 'I must get out of this damned place.' Of course, the kind of inhuman, brutalizing treatment practiced in the French penal colonies in those days added to his desire to be free. My name could easily have been Papillon too."

Released in December 1973, *Papillon* was a domestic and international hit. Though initial reviews were negative, over time it has been recognized as a classic and McQueen's acting tour de force.

> "MCQUEEN, THE ULTIMATE MOVIE ESCAPE HERO, WOULD BE MATCHED WITH THE ULTIMATE ESCAPE STORY."
>
> —MCQUEEN BIOGRAPHER MARSHALL TERRILL

EXPANDING THE LEGACY

JUNIOR BONNER

In 1971, a battered McQueen was looking for a change-of-pace role: his marriage to Neile was in ruins; his production company, Solar, was closed; and he had survived the financial debacle of his labor of love, the race car movie *Le Mans*. He found what he was looking for as the title character in *Junior Bonner*, an elegiac, low-key, character-driven drama about a way of life being shoved aside to make way for the future.

Junior "J. R." Bonner is an over-the-hill rodeo champion returning home to Prescott, Arizona, hoping for one last shot at glory and reconciliation with his estranged family. The director? The hard-living, hard-drinking, womanizing Sam Peckinpah, whose disruptive behavior had gotten him fired off *The Cincinnati Kid*. In an interview announcing the film, Steve told a reporter, "I know that I've been a big pain to the studios. I've always been a perfectionist, and that means I give headaches to a lot of people. Sam's got a bad rep too. He's a prime hellraiser. Him and me, we're *some* combo. ABC [the production company] is buyin' a lot of aspirin."

True to form, there were flare-ups and ego clashes, yet by Peckinpah standards, it was an amicable set that finished shooting in seven weeks. It was released in August 1972.

Critics were impressed. Some called McQueen's acting in it "one of his finest performances." Kathleen Carroll of the *New York Daily News* wrote, "McQueen has met with a role that fits him like a glove." Los Angeles film critic Michael Sragow wrote, "As a rodeo star past his prime, McQueen acts out faded glory without self-pity or preening. He displays just enough of his character's former vanity

> "IF YOU REALLY WANT TO LEARN ABOUT ACTING FOR THE SCREEN, WATCH MCQUEEN'S EYES."
>
> —DIRECTOR SAM PECKINPAH

and power to make his current failure sting. . . . He embodies Bonner so
fully, from the inside out, that when he
bandages up his damaged midsection
he seems to be struggling physically
to repair his pride. Few mainstream
American stars could pull off such a
balancing act." Calling it his favorite film, McQueen later said, "I liked
Junior Bonner very much. It was the
first time I'd worked with Sam, and
we got it together. I thought the script
was tremendous—one of the best
properties I've come across."

But, as a result of bad timing (in addition to *Junior Bonner*, three other
rodeo films had been released within
the span of three months) and bad
marketing (it was publicity touted it
as an action film, which it certainly
wasn't), it tanked. McQueen and
Peckinpah's next collaboration, however, would turn out better.

THE GETAWAY

> **"HE RADIATED SUCH MACHO ENERGY. MEN WANTED TO BE LIKE HIM. UPTIGHT SOCIETY LADIES AND BIKER MOLLS DIED TO BE WITH HIM."**
>
> **—COSTAR ALI MACGRAW**

In *Bullitt*, McQueen played a loner police detective and drove a souped-up Mustang to box-office glory. Four years later, in 1972, he bookended that action film with one even more explosive, as hardcore criminal Carter "Doc" McCoy in *The Getaway*, directed by Sam Peckinpah.

At the risk of oversimplification, *The Getaway* is an over-the-top violent road trip, the result of a corrupt politician (Ben Johnson) double-crossing McCoy and his wife (Ali MacGraw), who had agreed to split 50-50 the money they took in a bank heist in return for the politician's help in paroling McCoy

from jail for a previous crime. On the run with the police on their trail and after a wild series of increasingly violent plot twists and turns, the McCoys successfully escape to Mexico with their loot. In short, it was a classic Peckinpah film, but without the horses. As Peckinpah himself joked, "They've finally allowed me to work with cars and trains instead of horse and buggies."

Ali MacGraw was initially afraid to accept the role of Carol McCoy. For one thing, she didn't like the idea of playing a crime moll. For another, she was afraid of her passion for McQueen. Despite being married and a mother, she knew that in accepting the role, she'd leap into bed with the divorced McQueen and that her marriage would end as well.

MacGraw recalled that when she arrived for her first day of shooting on location in Texas, she was met by McQueen and Peckinpah and driven by McQueen back to the condominiums rented for the shoot. "What a drive! Steve was showing off, and the first thing this ex-Formula 1 race car driver did was to spin the rented car in a

dizzying loop across the four lanes of the freeway. It was a prophetic start to our relationship."

Affairs between cast members during a production are standard fare in Hollywood. Different versions exist on whether it happened immediately or after a few weeks. Regardless of the timetable, the result was as MacGraw predicted: she wound up in McQueen's bed, and their electric sexual attraction fairly leaps off the screen.

Their affair led to one of the more emotionally revealing moments in the film. In the final scene, when McQueen and MacGraw hitch a ride across the Mexican border from a local (Slim Pickens), Peckinpah pulled Pickens aside and told him to ad-lib some dialogue to "see what they can do." Pickens obliged, asking, "Are you kids married?" It was a moment that sparked real emotion from the two. McQueen's face registered shock. MacGraw gave a small smile and said, "Yes." Peckinpah remembered, "When Slim asked them if they were married, it really threw them badly. But they stayed with it, and it worked."

ALI MACGRAW

McQueen first met Ali MacGraw at a post–Academy Award party in 1971, about a year after his divorce from Neile. MacGraw was then married to studio head Robert Evans and had a son with him. But it was at a meeting to discuss her taking the lead role in *The Getaway* that they got to know each other and where the emotional sparks were ignited. McQueen so bowled over MacGraw that at one point she later confessed, "I had to leave the room to compose myself. He walked into my life as Mr. Humble, no ego, one of the guys. Steve was this very original, principled guy who didn't seem to be part of the system, and I loved that. He was clever, demure, exciting, and had all the answers. I bought that act in the first second. We had this electrifying, obsessive attraction."

MacGraw was reluctant to take the part, not so much because she was uncomfortable with playing the role of a moll (though that part was true), but because of something else. She later confessed, "The real reason I had hesitated was that I knew I was going to get in some serious trouble with Steve. There would be no avoiding it. He was recently separated and free, and I

was scared of my own overwhelming attraction to him."

She did take the role of Carol McCoy in *The Getaway* and, as she predicted, the affair commenced once she got on location in Texas. In 1972, MacGraw divorced Evans. Not long after that, she and McQueen moved in together in a beach house in Trancas, California.

THE TOWERING INFERNO

Producer Irwin Allen earned the nickname "Master of Disaster" for his high-powered, special-effects-laden, star-studded disaster films in the 1970s. He created the genre with *The Poseidon Adventure* (1972). His—and the genre's—crowning achievement was *The Towering Inferno* (1974), the story of a dedication ceremony for the world's tallest skyscraper in San Francisco gone horribly wrong.

On the night of the dedication and as a publicity stunt, all the lights in the tower are turned on. This causes an electrical overload, shorting out the system on the eighty-first floor, igniting a fire that quickly gets out of control, trapping the many celebrants, including political figures and high-powered business people, in the Promenade Room above. Steve McQueen had the role of San Francisco Fire Department 5th Battalion Chief Michael "Mike" O'Halloran. Sharing top billing with him in the role of Doug Roberts, the skyscraper's architect, was the actor with whom he had worked only once before, when McQueen was a bit actor in *Somebody Up There Likes Me*: Paul Newman.

Originally offered the role of architect Roberts, with his instinct for the more dramatic and pivotal role—

and after conferring with ex-wife Neile, always his most reliable and trusted sounding board—he chose the fire chief's role even though O'Halloran didn't appear until the movie's midpoint. As a result, even though he didn't have direct say in the matter, McQueen's decision opened the door for Newman.

Together in a movie for the first time as equals, McQueen made sure it was a situation taken literally, right down to the number of lines of dialogue. After tallying up Newman's lines and discovering that Newman's character had twelve more than his own, McQueen had the studio fetch screenwriter Sterling Silliphant away from his weekend yacht voyage and add twelve extra lines of O'Halloran dialogue.

Friendly rivals throughout their careers, the two displayed mutual respect and professionalism on the set, enjoying lighter moments together when not in front of the camera. But McQueen's competitive nature made sure that he had the movie's last word, literally.

In the final scene, Newman and McQueen are together doing a postmortem on the steps of the ruined skyscraper. O'Halloran states, "You

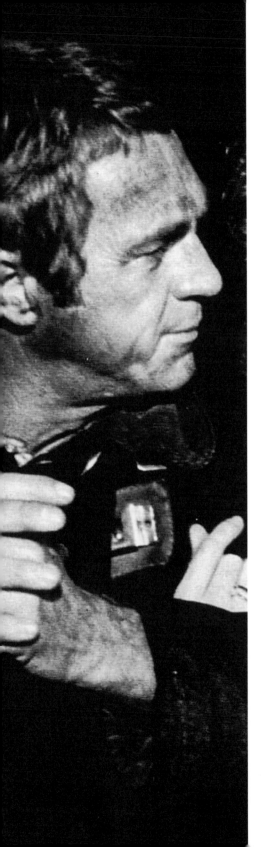

know, they'll keep building them higher and higher. And I'll keep eatin' smoke until one of you guys asks us how to build 'em." Roberts replies, "Okay, I'm asking." The fire chief replies, "You know where to find me. So long, architect." Game, set, and match to McQueen.

The Los Angeles Fire Department assigned a firefighter to each cast member of the film. For McQueen, his advisor was Battalion Chief Peter Lucarelli. During a meeting to discuss technical details, Lucarelli received a report of a major fire at the Goldywn Studio. Lucarelli suggested McQueen follow him, saying, "Maybe you can learn something."

Upon reaching the scene, McQueen donned firefighting gear and wound up joining a team that was hosing down a fiery ceiling. One of the firefighters did a double-take upon seeing the famous actor. "My wife will never believe this!" he said. McQueen smiled and replied, "Neither will mine." In August 1974, in an official ceremony at Los Angeles City Hall, McQueen was made an "honorary Los Angeles firefighter."

Released in December 1974, it was McQueen's biggest film ever, grossing an eye-popping $116 million in its first year and winning three Academy Awards. McQueen's percentage of the gross ensured that he was financially set for life.

PAUL NEWMAN

One of the most famous rivalries in Hollywood was that between McQueen and Paul Newman. Were they friendly rivals or just plain rivals? So much during their lives and since their deaths has been made of it that it's impossible to know for sure. One thing we do know is that though they never raced directly against each other, the rivalry extended beyond the silver screen and onto the racetrack.

Anecdotes abound showing that they could be friendly and comfortable around each other. In one early tale, shortly after the world premiere of *The Sand Pebbles* in 1966, the McQueens hosted a party in their Brentwood home where in addition to Hollywood A-listers Newman and James Garner, McQueen's motorcycle buddies, such as Bud Ekins, and other racers attended.

At one point, McQueen complained to Newman, "I'm due early to finish reading a new batch of scripts they just laid on me. Guess how many shitty scripts I've looked at in the last three months?"

"You tell me," Newman replied.

"One hundred and two! These scripts—they just keep comin' . . . more every day."

Newman smiled, mock punched McQueen on the shoulder, and said, "Hey, pal, the time to worry is when they *stop* coming!"

AN ENEMY OF THE PEOPLE

An Enemy of the People was a project that didn't come to him—McQueen went to it. Bored with the standard Hollywood fare he was being sent, once *The Towering Inferno* was finished, McQueen decided to retire. But after a couple years of boredom set in, he decided to do something different in film. That "something different" was a doozy: *An Enemy of the People*, a movie based on Arthur Miller's 1950 adaptation of Henrik Ibsen's 1882 play.

A political metaphor about a resort town in crisis after it discovers its source of income, a scenic well, is contaminated, it was the opposite of everything that McQueen's movie persona was. But performing in a classic piece of literature was why McQueen wanted to do it.

A great international cast that included Bibi Andersson and Charles Durning was assembled. For McQueen, *An Enemy of the People* represented the ultimate challenge for him as an actor, and he enthusiastically threw himself into the main role of Dr. Thomas Stockmann. But his labor of love proved to be anything but for the studio, First Artists, and distributor, Warner Bros. The short version: they didn't know what to do with it. The long version: they really didn't know what to do with it.

Instead of a McQueen action-adventure movie they knew they could sell, they had an against-type art house film. The picture was screened in select "preview" venues, where it was savaged by critics who, like the studio, didn't know how to respond to it. Warner Bros. never officially released it.

Though critics hated it, many of McQueen's peers were impressed by the movie. One those peers was Clint Eastwood. Eastwood was so taken by what McQueen had done that he told him, "You have the guts and the courage that I don't. I would love to be able to leave a classic behind, but I can't."

Years later, shortly after McQueen died, the film's director, George Schaefer, received a request from the Ibsen Society of America asking for a print of the film to show its membership. Schaefer attended the screening with some trepidation. "I was trembling," he recalled, "because I thought they might light into it. On the contrary, they were impressed with the performances, and the look and the wardrobe and the whole flavor of it. I think we did all we could with it, considering the budget we had. I think Steve accomplished what he wanted to do. It got some nice reactions. . . ."

TOM HORN

McQueen said, "I really feel this is my destiny to tell the true story of Tom Horn." If *An Enemy of the People* was a labor of love for McQueen, *Tom Horn* was a different sort of love; of all the characters he played, it was Tom Horn with whom he most identified. McQueen's interest in Horn was arguably to the point of obsession. Once he spent the night at Horn's gravesite in Columbia Cemetery in Boulder, Colorado. He later claimed to have had a visitation with Horn's ghost, saying, "I could feel him under there. It was like he said to me, 'Please do my story. Please tell my story.'"

Tom Horn was a legend who had the misfortune of outliving his time. He was a hero, a skilled army scout who fought against the Apache and helped track down and capture Geronimo and fought in the Spanish-American War. After the war, Horn returned to the West to find it irrevocably changed, with the frontier fenced in and cattlemen locked in a series of feuds and range wars. Hired as a range detective (hit man) for the ranchers, Horn proved too good at the job. Worried over political fallout, his employers had him framed for the murder of a thirteen-year-old boy. Tried and convicted, after several appeals, he was hanged on October 1, 1903.

Though the production was plagued by problems, including studio politics that slashed the original budget by more than 60 percent, McQueen's passion for being true to Tom Horn kept him focused and resulted in a bravura performance. Longtime friend James Coburn acknowledged this, stating, "*Tom Horn*, I thought, was Steve's best movie. He was loose and free, and he wasn't guarded. Most of his films he was guarded. He had a form. If the film wasn't rigid enough, he was going to be good. I always felt that Steve would really be a good actor if he ever grew up. . . . I think he finally did on *Tom Horn*. That was him finding his adulthood."

Tom Horn was released in 1980. Like the man on whom it was based, the movie's time had passed. Westerns were no longer in vogue. Coupled with mixed critical reviews and a misguided publicity campaign, it soon faded. It's since become regarded as a classic full of quiet, moody grace that successfully captured the end of an era that was the Old West at the turn of the twentieth century.

THE HUNTER

McQueen became a star telling the story of fictional Old West bounty hunter Josh Randall in the television series *Wanted: Dead or Alive*. His career came full circle with *The Hunter*, a movie based on the exploits of real-life modern-day bounty hunter Ralph "Papa" Thorson.

McQueen was fascinated by Thorson's hair-raising and dangerous career, during which he'd been shot twice, stabbed three times, and beaten more times than he could remember. After reading Thorson's biography and talking to him on the phone, McQueen said, "There's a hell of a picture here."

As might be expected, the movie is filled with all manner of chase scenes as McQueen tracks down and captures his quarry. One particularly wild scene involves a car-and-combine romp through a cornfield, in which McQueen's rental car is ultimately totaled. The dinged-up and/or wrecked conditions of McQueen's many cars in the movie became a running gag inspired by Thorson himself.

Thorson had a cameo as a bartender in the movie. Following the day's shoot, McQueen and Thorson went to a bar to have a drink, with Thorson driving. It turned out Thorson was a bad driver who had a hell of a problem parallel parking. Director Buzz Kulik said, "We had Steve in an old dented Chevy. Had him constantly bumping curbs and fenders. . . . Steve *loved* the idea of playing a lousy driver."

Released in August 1980, McQueen hoped *The Hunter* would be his comeback vehicle, as he had been out of the spotlight for a couple of years—an eternity in the entertainment industry. *The Hunter* was profitable, but only modestly so. More importantly, it would prove to be McQueen's last film.

...ot as fast...
...s what makes him human...
...a bounty hunter...
...hat's what makes him dangerous.

STEVE McQUEE

THE HUNTE

KAREN WILSON

McQueen met Karen Wilson in Chicago during the ten-day shooting of the climactic chase scene for *The Hunter*. McQueen spotted the feisty sixteen-year-old at the edge of a crowd that had gathered to watch the filming and tapped her to be one of the extras they needed that day. At the end of the day, McQueen asked her how she was going to spend her check. Wilson's answer floored him. "I'm going to give it to my mom. She's real sick." McQueen had her story checked out and discovered that Wilson's mother was dying.

McQueen arranged to visit Wilson's mother in the hospital, located in one of Chicago's toughest neighborhoods. "Is there anything I can do for you?" he asked. She replied, "All my life I wanted my daughter to go to school. I could die a happy woman knowing my daughter had a way out of this slum." McQueen promised her that she wouldn't have to worry. He'd take care of her daughter. Legal arrangements were made for McQueen and his third wife, Barbara Minty, to be her legal guardian. After shooting for *The Hunter* was finished, the McQueens took her with them to California and raised her, enrolling her in a private school.

She later said, "It amazes me. There I was . . . a nobody. . . . I had so little and now I have so much. My whole life has been turned around by this man. He came and—boom! Thanks to Steve McQueen, my life has a new beginning."

Barbara said that after McQueen died, she continued to look after her and said, "Karen is now a happily married mother of four kids."

> ## "I FOUND HIM TO BE EXTREMELY CAUTIOUS ABOUT FRIENDSHIP, ABOUT ALLOWING PEOPLE TO ENTER HIS LIFE. YOU HAD TO SUSTAIN THE RELATIONSHIP ON HIS TERMS."
>
> ## —*SAND PEBBLES* CO-STAR RICHARD CRENNA

RACING TO LIVE

RACING TO PAY THE BILLS

In between acting lessons and minor roles that paid little money, during the 1950s, McQueen took all manner of odd jobs, including dishwasher, truck driver, and even boxer to make ends meet. One of his more reliable sources of income was motorcycle racing, whether legally at the Long Island City Raceway across the East River in Queens (where he regularly pocketed the top purse of $100), or illegally along the wide boulevards in the outer boroughs of Queens and Brooklyn and the West Side Highway of Manhattan.

His racing bike during this period was a Harley-Davidson K Model, the company's sport bike and predecessor to the Sportster. Introduced in 1952, it was Harley-Davidson's most technologically advanced bike, with a new engine design that for the first time incorporated the engine and hand-operated clutch transmission in a single case. It was also the first H-D to incorporate modern hydraulic dampened suspension, with telescopic front forks and a rear suspension incorporating a swingarm and shock absorber.

The foot-operated gear shift and rear brake, though similar to that found on British bikes, was done less in imitation of them than it was for purposes of flat track racing. Depending on the year, engine sizes ranged from 45 to 52 cubic inches. The bikes were powerful and fast, and McQueen made the most of the K Model's speed.

> "RACING GAVE ME A FRESH IDENTITY. I WAS NO LONGER JUST AN ACTOR, I WAS A GUY WHO RACED. AND IT WAS REAL IMPORTANT TO ME—TO HAVE THIS SEPARATE IDENTITY."
>
> —STEVE MCQUEEN

ROOKIE CAR RACER

Southern California was a mecca for racing, and McQueen wanted to take his driving skills to the next level.

In 1959, he entered nine Sports Car Club of America races with his 1958 Porche Speedster. His first official race was May 30, 1959, the Preliminary Santa Barbara Competition. It was one of the few times he questioned his driving skills.

Of that first race, he recalled, "They ran it at the airport—and there was a real mix of cars, in my race. I remember storming off the line like mad when the flag fell, passing a gaggle of Porsches and Triumphs—until after about four laps there I was, leading everybody! That shook me. I was skidding around the circuit between cars, going as deep into the turns as possible before braking, on the ragged edge all the way, and I thought, 'Man, what are you *doing* out there?' But I hung on and won. After that, I was hooked."

In his second race, held later the same day, McQueen finished first in his class. It was a tremendous boost to his ego. He later said, "Racing gave me a fresh identity. I was no longer just an actor, I was a guy who raced. And it was real important to me—to have this separate identity."

BARBOUR INTERNATIONAL JACKET

Barbour's association with motorcycles began in 1936 with the "International," a racing jacket designed for the British national team for the International Six Days Trials (ISDT) endurance race. Dark green and made of wax cotton, the International was tough and waterproof and not only utilitarian, but also stylish. During World War II, Barbour supplied the Royal Navy's submariners with a slightly modified version of the International, the official Submarine Commanders coat. By the 1950s it was the jacket of choice for motorcycle racing teams around the world. McQueen, Ekins, and the rest of the US national team wore a version of the International called the "A7" when they competed in the 1964 ISDT held in what was then East Germany.

Photos of McQueen in his jacket made the International a hit with non-racers who wanted to be cool like McQueen. McQueen became so identified with the International that Barbour later came out with a line of authorized McQueen jackets that continue to be available today.

Another clothier whose biker jacket McQueen liked was Belstaff. McQueen wore its Trialmaster black biker jacket in *Bullitt*. In 2006, the company purchased the Trialmaster he wore in the movie for $35,000 and put it on display in its museum showroom in Milan, Italy.

> "I DIDN'T KNOW IF I WAS AN ACTOR WHO RACED OR A RACER WHO ACTED."
>
> —STEVE MCQUEEN

THE KING OF COOL'S RACE CARS

McQueen owned a number of race cars during his racing years. His "starter" car was a Porsche Speedster 1600 Super, which was soon replaced by a Porsche 356 Carrera. He quickly moved up from that to a more powerful Lotus XI. Pressure from studio bosses forced him to sell the Lotus and take a break from racing. It was a short-lived hiatus.

In between the filming of *The War Lover* in England, McQueen returned to the racetrack, competing at Brands Hatch in a Mini Cooper. During one race, he almost gave the studio heads a heart attack when he wound up in an accident that almost killed him. Luckily, he walked away from it with only minor injuries that wound up adding to the film's verisimilitude.

The Mini was followed by a Cooper T52 FJ and then a Porsche 908 that he drove at Sebring and later in *Le Mans*. But the one that stood apart was the off-road Baja Boot.

Designed by Vic Hickey (who would later assist in designing the Lunar Rover and the Humvee), the Baja Boot was a technologically advanced, mid-engine off-road "supercar." In addition, it contained a "give back" to racing from McQueen: the Baja Bucket seat. Concerned about driver injuries due to rollover, the Baja Bucket was a seat designed and patented in 1969 by McQueen to help prevent such injuries.

STIRLING MOSS

McQueen had few heroes, but one of them was British racing legend Stirling Moss.

Moss later recalled, "I met Steve back in 1959 in California. He was keen on racing bikes and cars, and he had heard that I was going to be at a particular race. I suppose in those days when you were in the know and somebody came to town, it was quite easy to track him down. Steve found out I was staying in Beverly Hills and invited me to stay with him and his wife, Neile. At the time, I'd never heard of Steve, but he was so friendly and persuasive, it was hard to say no."

Their shared love of fast cars forged a bond that grew to a point where he became a family friend. When McQueen went to England to work on *The War Lover*, he promptly contacted Moss, who arranged for McQueen to be a part of the British Motor Corporation team racing Mini Coopers and gave him instructions in how to navigate the circuits at Aintree, Oulton Park, and Brands Hatch, where McQueen suffered what nearly became a fatal accident.

In 1962, while recovering from a near-fatal accident of his own that ended his career, Moss jauntily wrote a letter to McQueen telling him that his upcoming film, *The Great Escape*, "sounds as though it could be good." He deprecatingly added, "Unfortunately I am not sure that Neile will still love me because I am a bit broken up. . . . However, please tell her that I still love her."

> "HE IMPRESSED ME AS A FELLOW WHO BELIEVED IN ACTION. HE WAS VERY KEEN TO LEARN EVERYTHING HE COULD ABOUT HIGH-SPEED MOTOR RACING. HE'D LISTEN CAREFULLY, TAKE ADVICE, AND WAS A QUICK LEARNER."
>
> —STIRLING MOSS

PETER REVSON

In preparation for *Le Mans*, McQueen wanted to get in some Grand Prix–style racing experience. He entered his Porsche Spyder team in the 12 Hours of Sebring to be held in March 1970. The format called for each driver to alternate for ninety minutes behind the wheel. For his codriver, McQueen chose thirty-one-year-old Peter Revson. Revson was handsome, rich, an heir to the Revlon cosmetics dynasty, and a consummate ladies' man, and McQueen found a kindred spirit in him. More importantly, Revson was a ranked Formula 1 driver who had some impressive finishes in his career. They would need all the skills at their disposal, and then some, because they'd be competing against Jo Siffert/Brian Redman (Gulf-Porsche), Jacky Ickx/Peter Schetty (Ferrari), and Mario Andretti/Arturo Merzario (Ferrari), among other top drivers. The "then some" came as a result of McQueen having broken his foot in a motorcycle accident while racing in the Third Annual Elsinore Grand Prix.

The 1970 12 Hours of Sebring is regarded by many experts as the best ever. Andretti immediately took the lead, and he and Siffert kept battling for position. But the combination of Revson and McQueen was not to be dismissed, even with McQueen's left foot in a cast. Mechanical problems saw other cars dropping out of the race one by one, and by nightfall, the McQueen and Revson Solar Productions/Gulf Porsche was in third place. With about thirty minutes remaining, Revson took advantage of an Andretti pit stop to take over first place.

But, even though there was just one lap to go, Andretti roared out of the pit stop in his five-liter Ferrari as the two cars were closing on the finish line, and with seconds remaining, Andretti managed to narrowly take the lead and win. McQueen/Revson would take first in their three-liter class and second overall.

Revson would go on to win the 1973 British Grand Prix and the 1973 Canadian Grand Prix. On March 22, 1974, while racing in the South African Grand Prix, his Shadow-Ford suffered suspension failure, and he died in the crash at age thirty-five. Peter Windsor, Grand Prix editor for *F1 Racing*, wrote, "Revson could have become a genuine American sporting superstar. Instead, he died—and remains—a genuine American hero."

LE MANS

"I HONESTLY BELIEVE THAT HAD STEVE PURSUED A CAREER IN RACING RATHER THAN SHOW BUSINESS, HE PROBABLY COULD HAVE MADE A LIVING AT IT."

—PORSCHE RACE CAR MECHANIC HAIG ALLTOUNIAN

"I've always wanted to shoot a motor racing picture because it's always been something close to my heart," McQueen said. "And, sometimes I thought, well, maybe I shouldn't do it. When it's something this close to you, you have a tendency to become too much of a perfectionist with it." Producer and friend Robert Relyea said, "It had always been in Steve's mind that if you are going to make a racing picture, you make it about one race, Le Mans."

The 24 Hours of Le Mans is the world's oldest and most storied race.

It's one leg of the Triple Crown of Motorsport, the other two being the Indianapolis 500 and the Monaco Grand Prix. Its Grand Prix format makes it a grueling test of speed and endurance for both car and driver. At the pinnacle of his career, McQueen had the power to pull out all stops for *Le Mans*, and he did. Shortly after *The Great Escape*, in 1963 McQueen formed the independent production company Solar Productions. Though he did other films over the years through Solar, McQueen created it with one overarching purpose in mind: to produce a racing film. Finally, in 1970, he was able to achieve that dream.

Le Mans included a mix of authentic race cars and stock cars customized for specific requirements in the movie. Drivers included such racing professionals as past Le Mans winners Jacky Ickx and Richard Attwood. Special camera rigs were installed on the front and back of a Porsche 917 for shooting race sequences. A Ford GT40 did additional camera-car duty. Scouting and archival shooting of an actual Le Mans race was done a year before to find the best locations for setting up the camera and to get the semi-documentary look that McQueen wanted. But while every effort was done to make the

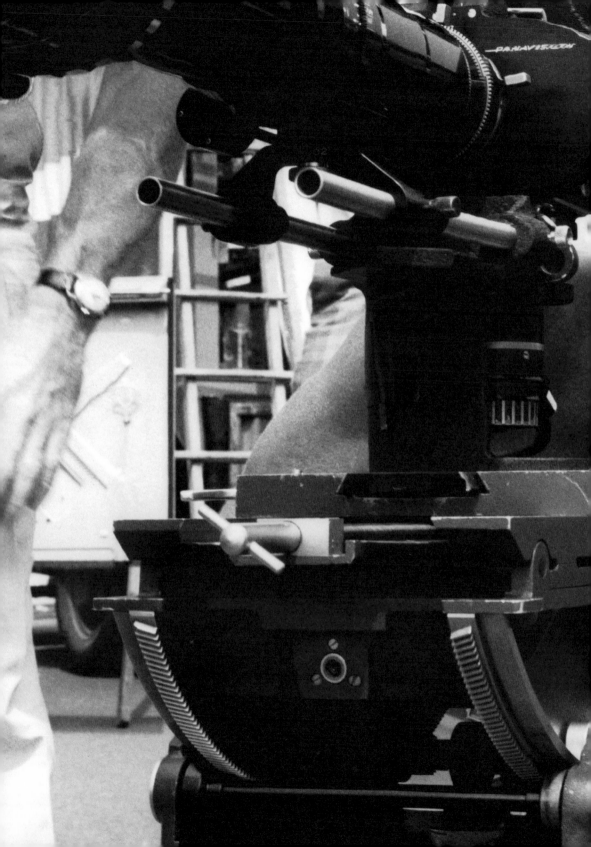

race realistic, similar effort was all but ignored regarding the script. Production began without one.

The skeletal plot is about the competition between the Porsche team, led by Michael Delaney (McQueen), and rival Ferrari team, led by Erich Stahler (Siegfried Rauch). Elga Andersen plays Lisa Belgetti, the widow of a driver killed in the previous year's race in an accident involving Delaney.

Ironically, with *Le Mans*, McQueen, the most American of actors, created a film containing enough tropes to make it an existential homage to the movies of Goddard and Truffaut. But the American audience didn't want a thought-provoking French New Wave film, they wanted another *Bullitt*.

Released in 1971, *Le Mans* bombed at the box office, bankrupted Solar, and wrecked his marriage to Neile. The one redeeming factor was praise for it being an accurate depiction of auto racing and remains so to this day—the whole reason why McQueen wanted to do the movie.

McQueen said, "I laid the whole package on the line for that one—my career, my money, my marriage, even my life. I went balls out on *Le Mans*."

BELL HELMET

Whether on a motorcycle or in a race car, McQueen's helmet of choice was made by Bell, the preeminent helmet manufacturer of the 1960s and 1970s.

Founded in 1954 by Roy Richter, a former race car driver who named the company after the town where he had his first shop (Bell, California), Richter became passionate about racing safety after a close friend died in a racing accident. The company started out supplying open-face helmets for race car drivers and law enforcement agencies. Though motorcyclists purchased Bell helmets, the company did not begin producing full-face motorcycle helmets until 1971.

For the 1964 ISDT, McQueen wore an open-face Bell Jet RT painted in the US national team colors, a blue shell accented with red and white stripes and a white snap-on visor.

When he was racing in off-road competitions on his motorcycles, he often wore a black open-face Santa Monica Bell helmet, with a gold pinstripe trim designed by his friend Von Dutch.

In the famous August 23, 1971, cover photo of *Sports Illustrated*, McQueen is putting on a show, bare-chested with his head capped by a snow-white Bell helmet, popping a wheelie on his Husqvarna 400 Cross.

Sports Illustrated

AUGUST 23, 1971   60 CENTS

STEVE McQUEEN
ESCAPES
ON
WHEELS

MOTORCYCLE SPORT AND THE MEN WHO RIDE ON ANY SUNDAY

A FILM BY BRUCE BROWN

ON ANY SUNDAY

Starting with the release of *The Wild One* in 1953, the general public had a negative impression of motorcyclists and motorcycle racing, something that rankled McQueen. In a 1971 issue of *Sports Illustrated* McQueen said, "Most bike flicks in the past concentrated on the outlaw crap, Hell's Angels and all of that stuff, which is about as far away from the real world of motorcycle racing as I am from Lionel Barrymore."

After the success of his surfing documentary *The Endless Summer*, Bruce Brown began looking around for another subject to shoot. That led him to the motorcycle racing culture in Southern California. "I met a few of the racers and was struck by how approachable and how nice most of these guys were," he recalled. "It wasn't at all like the image a lot of people had about motorcycle riders in those days. I just thought it would be neat to do a movie about motorcycle racing and the people involved."

Aware of McQueen's interest in the sport, Brown arranged a meeting with McQueen and pitched his idea. McQueen loved it and asked what part Brown wanted him to play. Brown said he wanted McQueen

to finance it. McQueen laughed and said he didn't finance films, he acted in them. Brown jokingly replied, "Alright, then, you can't be in the movie." The next day Brown got a phone call from McQueen. He agreed to back it.

On Any Sunday told the story of motorcycle racing and riding in its many forms through the story of three riders, McQueen, Malcolm Smith, and Mert Lawwill. They all knew each other and were friends. Malcolm recalled, "Shooting the ending sequences [on the beach at Camp Pendleton] was a lot of fun. The scenes themselves—riding with your friends, cow trailing, beach riding, sliding around, goofing off—really did capture the essence of the fun of motorcycling, and Bruce did a masterful job recording it for eternity. Steve was very competitive and always wanted to be out front, which worked well for the cow-pie [scene]. The shots of Mert flinging cow poo off his arm, of me laughing, and of Steve looking back at us with an evil grin are epic."

On Any Sunday was a critical and commercial success that transformed the image of motorcycles and motorcycle racing.

TRIUMPH BONNEVILLE DESERT SLED

McQueen knew about the desert-modified Triumphs resting in the back of Bud Ekins's motorcycle shop. But it took seeing fellow actor Keenan Wynn racing up a cliff full throttle for him to get the bug. McQueen's first off-road bike was a 500cc Triumph Tiger bought from Ekins, who agreed to take him out and "show him the ropes" of desert riding. It wasn't long before McQueen was good enough to go for an upgrade.

Back then, little differentiated stock street and off-road bikes from each other. The most notable differences were in the placement of the exhaust pipes, tires, and handlebars. For serious hare 'n' hound riders, bikes had to be custom built from the bottom up. McQueen's customized dirt bike began as a stock Triumph Bonneville T120.

While Bud and his staff, including Bud's brother, Dave, tore apart and rebuilt the bike, Kenny "Von Dutch" Howard worked on painting the gas tank and side covers. Because of the bike's intended use, Von Dutch opted against doing anything fancy, instead going for an unadorned olive-green paint job. The result of their handiwork was a classic Triumph Desert Sled, which would become the motorcycle most associated with McQueen.

> "YOU DON'T LIE ABOUT THE SPORT. AND YOU DON'T CHEAT AT IT. YOU PLAY IT STRAIGHT. I BROKE A SHOULDER AND I BROKE AN ARM IN TWO PLACES AND I HAD FOUR STITCHES IN MY HEAD, ALL BEFORE THESE PEOPLE ACCEPTED ME FOR REAL. FINALLY I CONVINCED THEM I WASN'T OUT THERE FOR PUBLICITY OR FOR LAUGHS. I WAS OUT THERE TO WIN."
>
> —STEVE MCQUEEN

HUSQVARNA 400 CROSS

> ## "I'D RATHER RUN A FAST BIKE OVER CLEAN DESERT THAN DO ANYTHING ELSE IN THE WORLD."
>
> ## —STEVE MCQUEEN

For many years, McQueen's go-to off-road motorcycle was the Triumph 650. But while the four-stroke powerplant had the muscle, it was also a monster, heavy and challenging to maneuver in the rugged desert terrain. Then, sometime in the late 1960s or early 1970s, he wrapped his legs around a Husky and a whole new world of fun opened up.

Light and nimble, with a two-stroke engine that delivered breathtaking power and a bright red and chrome gas tank, the Husky was a two-wheeled off-road rocket. For McQueen, it was love at first sight. After people saw him racing and riding the Husky 400 Cross in the motorcycle documentary *On Any Sunday*, sales shot through the roof.

In February 2008, Husky enthusiast Rob Phillips purchased for $1,500 a 1970 Husqvarna 400 that he planned to restore. After doing a background check of paperwork to learn the history of his acquisition, he discovered that his Husky wasn't just another bike.

The original sales invoice dated February 9, 1970, together with confirmation from the Manufacturer's Statement of Origin, revealed that the first owner of his Husky was McQueen and that it was likely (though it couldn't be confirmed) one he rode in *On Any Sunday*. In 1984, a McQueen 1971 Husky 400 Cross was sold at auction for $144,500. Phillips's little weekend project turned out to be the jackpot.

BUD AND DAVE EKINS

Bud Ekins had a Triumph dealership in Sherman Oaks, California, in 1959 when he met McQueen. Ekins had sold a Triumph Bonneville to Norman Powell, the son of Dick Powell, the head of Four Star Productions, which was producing *Wanted: Dead or Alive*. "Steve . . . would come into my shop riding on the back [of the bike] with Norm. Well, one day, Norm said that he'd sold the bike to Steve and was wondering if the warranty was still good. I said, 'Sure, no problem.'" Thus, as the saying goes, was "the beginning of a beautiful friendship."

Though some of his customers were Hollywood celebrities, Bud's brother, Dave, wrote in *McQueen's Motorcycles*, "Bud was not especially impressed with the Hollywood scene, so it was easy for celebrities to come and go as they pleased without any special attention brought to them."

Once they got to know each other, the Ekins brothers introduced McQueen to off-road racing. "There was a camaraderie in the desert among Bud, Steve, and me," Dave added. "The courage it took to be an actor and to race was central to Steve McQueen's life: he put himself out there on the stage as an actor and also risked it all for the thrill of racing with a bunch of regular guys. He was one of us."

CHAPTER EIGHT

A LIFE IN STYLE

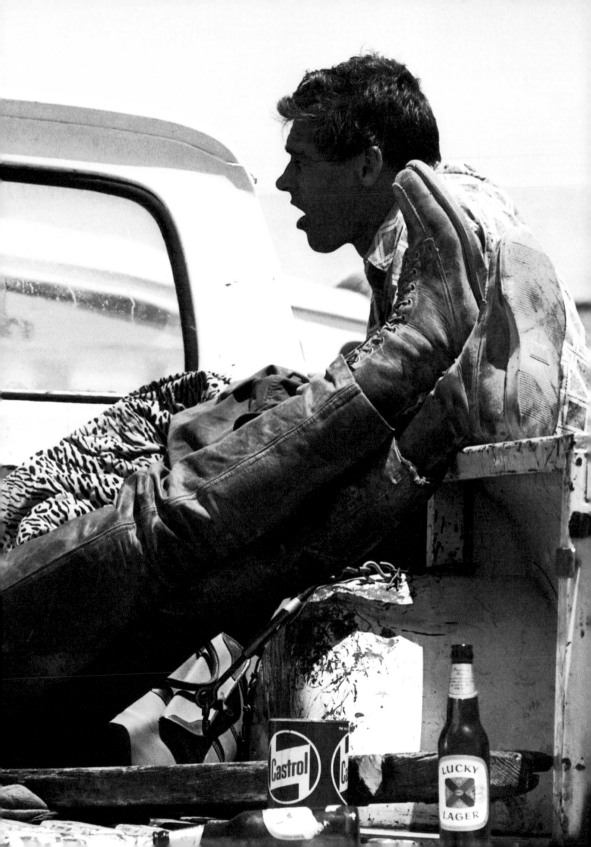

CALIFORNIA DREAMING:
THE HOME ON SOLAR DRIVE

In 1960, McQueen, Neile, and their daughter, Terry, moved into a midcentury home on Solar Drive in Palm Springs. It was strategically placed on Nichols Canyon Ridge with views of Runyon Canyon and the valley on one side and the Pacific Ocean on the other. Its narrow access street and poorly marked signage gave it a sense of isolation amongst the bustle of the city below.

The 3,600-square-foot house had three bedrooms and was built in the post and beam design and featured a low-slung flat roof that was then in fashion. Its open floor plan, lack of ornamentation, and geometric aesthetic gave it a spacious look.

In 1963, McQueen allowed *Life* magazine photographer John Dominis to come into the house and take pictures. Forty rolls of photos were shot, and though most photos weren't used, fans still got a rare glimpse of the famous star at leisure with his wife, listening and dancing to jazz, relaxing beside the swimming pool, and working out in his private gym, among other activities.

The shoot lasted three weeks, and when his work was done, Dominis said, "They liked me, and they had a silver mug made: 'To John Dominis, for work beyond the call of duty.'"

NEILE ADAMS MCQUEEN

Ruby Neilam Salvador Adams, better known as Neile, was McQueen's first wife and the most important woman in his life after his mother. But unlike Jullian, Neile's influence was for the better. They met in New York City during the 1950s when he was a struggling actor and she a rising dance talent on television and Broadway. When they married, it was Neile who had the bigger career than McQueen, but after he became a television star, she set aside her career to be wife, mother, and advisor to her husband.

Neile was his most important advisor when it came to scripts and roles—a function she served even after they divorced. In addition to knowing what roles were right for him, she knew how to play him so that he'd take roles he initially turned down. Case in point: the title role in *The Thomas Crown Affair*.

"He didn't want it, but he didn't want anybody else to have it either," she recalled. Neile bided her time. Her moment came one morning while making French toast. She casually mentioned that director Norman Jewison didn't want McQueen for the movie. Puzzled,

McQueen asked why. "Well, you know Norman wants either Sean Connery or Rock Hudson for this part, and I just think it's unfortunate, because I think you could really be terrific in it. . . . He's given the script to everyone in Hollywood *but* you." Though she was right that Jewison *didn't* want McQueen, thinking he was completely wrong for the part, she knew better. His pride piqued, McQueen put in a call, arranged a meeting with the director, and convinced him.

Jewison later said, "I think he wanted to grow up; he wanted to play a part that he had never played before, and maybe, in a secret desire deep within him, he wanted to be Thomas Crown." McQueen admitted, "This dude wants to show he can beat the establishment at its own game. He's essentially a rebel, like me. Sure, a high society rebel, but he's my kind of cat. It was just that his outer fur was different—so I got me some fur."

As Neile predicted, McQueen proved perfect for the part.

GETTING PHYSICAL

It's impossible to be cool if you don't look good. And McQueen knew that looking good was only possible if he stayed in good physical shape. Thanks to his acting and racing, he carried the double burden of not only having to look good, but also of being in top physical shape. The latter applied not only to racing but to his acting career as well, as he insisted on doing his own stunts.

McQueen was obsessed with being fit. When he moved in with Neile in New York City, among his meagre possessions was a New York City street sign that he used as a barbell. McQueen didn't work out to gain muscles—he wanted a lithe, lean, sculpted look that comes from swimming, boxing, and martial arts.

Martial artist and actor Bruce Lee taught McQueen his jeet kune do martial arts program in exchange for acting lessons. He described a typical McQueen session: "One day I went to his place to work out and that guy doesn't know the meaning of quitting. He just kept pushing himself for hours—punching and kicking without a break—until he was completely exhausted. His gym clothes were completely soaked by the time we gave up."

COOL JAZZ

During his photo shoot of McQueen in his Solar Drive home, *Life* photographer John Dominis saw something he didn't expect: McQueen's extensive collection of jazz records. Scattered on the carpeted floor and stacked beside his record player were albums by a wide range of greats: Miles Davis, John Coltrane, Milt Jackson, John Lewis, Count Basie, Paul Horn, Sonny Rollins, and more. It was yet another side to what biographer Marshall Terrill called "the most multi-faceted and complex person I ever researched."

It was during the 1950s while living and rubbing shoulders with the art colony in Greenwich Village that McQueen got exposed to a different lifestyle. He later said, "For the first time in my life I was really exposed to music, culture, a little kindness, a little sensitivity. It was a way of life where people talk out their problems instead of punching you."

Though Jim Marshall was famous for his photos of 1960s rock stars, his first love was jazz. In 1963 at the Monterey Jazz Festival, he captured an iconic photo of McQueen with Miles Davis—the King of Cool in deep conversation with the Prince of Darkness.

THE KING OF COOL'S STREET CARS

When it comes to street cars, many are cool, but few are Cool with a capital C. McQueen had the touch that brought the cache of coolness to even such humble vehicles as the 1952 Chevrolet pickup he used for cross-country camping trips. And he had in his stable his share of Ferraris (275 GTS and 275 GTS/4 NART Spyder) and of course the Porsche 911S Coupe. But, arguably, his *coolest* car was his 1956 Jaguar XKSS. With a bona fide racing pedigree, painted in British Racing Green, and with the driver's side on the right (this being before the federal government mandated automaker conformity), the car looked great, sounded great, and drove great.

McQueen nicknamed it the "Green Rat" and, when he was acting in *Wanted: Dead or Alive*, would sometimes tie his horse to it.

The Green Rat was built for speed, and McQueen loved to drive it fast on Southern California's highways. Needless to say, this caused him to collect his share of speeding tickets and have his license suspended twice. He narrowly avoided a third suspension by claiming that he was racing to get to the hospital because then-pregnant Neile was in labor (she was actually only six months pregnant).

How do we know that the Jag was the coolest of McQueen's vehicles? He sold it in 1969 but wound up missing it so much that he bought it back in 1977.

"MCQUEEN DOMINATES EVERY SCENE. HIS PERFORMANCE IS ONE OF THE MOST AUTHORITATIVE OF HIS CAREER. ONCE AGAIN, AMID A STARRY CAST, MCQUEEN EMERGES AS THE OUTSIDER, EXISTING WITHIN HIS OWN SET OF PRINCIPLES AND BELIEFS."

—FILM HISTORIAN DEREK ELLEY

BRUCE LEE

When asked who among his famous jeet kune do martial arts clients was the best, Bruce Lee replied, "Depending, okay? As a fighter, Steve . . . Steve McQueen, now, he is good in that department because the son of a gun's has got the toughness in him. I mean, he would say, 'All right, baby, here I am, man,' you know? And he'll do it!"

Before he became an internationally famous martial arts movie star, Lee was a sometime actor (he was Kato in the short-lived television series *Green Hornet*) and instructor of jeet kune do, a martial arts style he created, whose A-list clients included James Coburn, James Garner, Kareem Abdul-Jabbar, and McQueen.

Racing and the fact that he tried to do his own stunts as much as possible meant McQueen had to be in top physical shape, and he was impressed with the wide range of demands Lee's regimen placed on the body and how it could benefit him in front of the camera. Lee said, "Most of [the actors], they are coming in to ask me not so much how to defend themselves, they want to learn to express themselves through movement, be it anger, be it determination, or whatsoever.

[McQueen] is paying me to show him in combative form, the art of expressing the human body."

Lee's taste of stardom in *Green Hornet* spurred him to continue his acting. He used McQueen as his bellwether and achieved his goal when he moved to Hong Kong to star in a series of martial arts films becoming, in his words, the "Oriental Steve McQueen." Lee achieved international screen immortality with the martial arts movie *Enter the Dragon*, which was released six days after his tragic death at age thirty-two in 1973.

Lee's death deeply touched McQueen. He told Lee's friend, fellow martial artist and Lee biographer Mitoshi Uyehara, "I cared about Bruce and I think it's going to be a great loss. I feel very bad about it. He was a wonderful guy." Though McQueen disliked attending funerals, he went to Seattle to be one of Lee's pallbearers, stating, "I felt like saying goodbye to a friend. That's why I went up there to pay respect and try to and make it easier on the people around him."

In 2016, Lee's four-page student profile of McQueen was sold at auction for $24,000.

CHUCK NORRIS

Chuck Norris was a champion karate competitor who had a dojo in Sherman Oaks when he met McQueen. McQueen's son, Chad, had been involved in a fight at school, and McQueen wanted his son to be able to defend himself. Bruce Lee recommended Norris, saying, "If you ever want to take karate lessons, Norris is the best."

Norris began giving private lessons to both father and son. Norris said, "Steve had excellent reflexes and natural athletic ability. He trained hard and was a born fighter. He was not afraid to mix it up with anybody. Once he made up his mind to do something, he went all out."

Norris pursued acting on the side and had his first starring role in *Breaker! Breaker!* (1977). After screening it, Norris thought it the worst movie he had ever seen. McQueen saw it and told Norris, "Well, it's not that bad of a film. But let me give you some advice. You are verbalizing things on the screen that we have already seen visually and movies are visual—a visual thing. Another thing, let your character actors fill in the plot of the movie. And when there's something important, very important for you to say, then you say it. Then people will remember what you say. That's what you've got to have in your movies. Memorable lines."

> "I SAW A MOVIE CALLED *ON ANY SUNDAY* AND I SAID IF THERE WAS ANY ONE ACTOR I'D LIKE TO MEET, THAT'S THE MAN I'D LIKE TO MEET."
>
> —CHUCK NORRIS ON STEVE MCQUEEN

BARBARA MINTY MCQUEEN

By 1977, McQueen's marriage to MacGraw was nearing its end. Meanwhile, McQueen had set his sights on another woman, fashion model Barbara Minty, and he used one of the oldest tricks in the Hollywood book to meet her. In July 1977, McQueen telephoned Minty's agent and said he had seen her in a magazine and wanted to give her a screen test for a role in a movie—a role that he knew didn't exist. The agent called Minty at her horse ranch in Idaho. Minty protested that she didn't know how to act. Her agent said, "I know, but it's a free trip to Los Angeles, and you never know what might happen. Maybe you'll get a small part in a movie." Minty went down, thinking that she was going to meet with Paul Newman because, amazingly, she didn't know who Steve McQueen was. When they met over lunch at the Beverly Wilshire Hotel, she found herself with a man with long hair and a beard who "seemed more like a beach bum than a movie star." The meeting lasted two hours, and Minty was smitten.

In November of that year, McQueen filed for divorce from MacGraw. Shortly after that, Minty moved in with him. A friend later said, "Barbara was a lot more into Steve's world than Ali ever was. Instead of asking him to take her to the ballet, she got tickets to a Rolling Stones rock concert in Anaheim. She and Steve were 'birds of a feather.' That old saying really fit them."

It's a point Minty agrees with. Reflecting on the time she spent hanging out and living in the airplane hangar that McQueen bought to store the bulk of his collection, she said, "I absolutely adored it. . . . We had everything we needed: a television, a bed, and a kitchen that was extremely small, which was fine with me, because I hate to cook.

"But how cool is it to wake up in the morning surrounded by airplanes, motorcycles, and tool chests? I was brought up on a dairy farm, and I'm not a girly girl. If I woke up in Paris Hilton's closet, I'd freak out!"

AN AMERICAN ICON
FOR MEN'S STYLE

JACK PURCELL CANVAS SNEAKERS

The white Jack Purcell canvas sneaker was one of McQueen's favorites. Designed by Canadian badminton champion Jack Purcell in 1935, the white canvas and rubber-soled shoe was designed to provide additional arch support and be sturdy enough for punishing play on the badminton court.

It also happened to look damned good off the court as well, and McQueen became one of the first Hollywood icons to lace up his feet in a pair.

"I LOOK AT STEVE MCQUEEN'S WARDROBE, WHICH HAS STAYED RELEVANT TO THIS DAY, AND I REMEMBER DOMENICO DOLCE'S QUOTE: 'WOMEN ARE INTO FASHION, MEN ARE INTO STYLE, STYLE IS FOREVER.'"

—CLASSIQ

BARACUTA G9 HARRINGTON JACKET

As the King of Cool and the epitome of the Hollywood antihero, McQueen knew how to look the part off screen as well. Like all masters of their crafts, McQueen paid close attention to his attire, down to the smallest detail, and made looking good seem effortless. His way of dressing casually has proved timeless and continues to influence men's fashion to this day.

> "BARACUTA'S FINEST MOMENT ARGUABLY ARRIVED . . . WHEN G9 LOVER STEVE MCQUEEN APPEARED IN *THE THOMAS CROWN AFFAIR* WEARING A NAVY BLUE VERSION OF THE MODEL."
>
> —"BARACUTA G9: THE HISTORY OF THE HARRINGTON," MASON & SONS

McQueen proved he could look great in anything and certain outfits became his trademark. Not surprisingly, one of the most memorable was his casual but stylish ensemble of denim jeans, a white T-shirt, and a Baracuta G9 Harrington jacket.

Invented in 1937 as a golf jacket (thus the G), McQueen was one of a handful of influential stars, including Elvis Presley (who introduced it to the mainstream American audience when he wore it in his 1958 film, *King Creole*), James Dean, and Frank Sinatra. The cover of the July 12, 1963, issue of *Life* magazine featured McQueen and his wife Neile riding one of his motorcycles. McQueen was wearing a G9, and sales of the windbreaker promptly shot through the ceiling. Though he wore them in a variety of colors, one stood out: pale blue-white. He was seen, and photographed, enough in that jacket color that it soon came to be named "McQueen Stone" and is available in that color today.

In 2007, Baracuta released a limited-edition line of 70th Anniversary Icon Baracuta G9 jackets: the Presley, the Sinatra, and the McQueen. Stitched on the inside label of each jacket was a quote from the famous performers. The quote in McQueen's is, "I live for myself."

THE KING OF COOL'S WATCHES

McQueen loved watches and accumulated an impressive collection during his lifetime. The watchmakers ranged from very high end, including Switzerland's Patek Philippe and Rolex, Germany's Hanhart, and France's Cartier, to modest American makers such as Gruen and Benrus.

Far and away his most famous watch was the Heuer Monaco, which was featured prominently in *Le Mans*. Ironically, it was a one-off wear; he only wore that distinctive chronograph with its square case and blue-and-white dial for the movie.

The other watchmaker most associated with McQueen is Rolex. His favorite everyday watch was the Submariner 5512, which he wore in *The Towering Inferno* and *The Hunter*. He so liked it and the 5513 that he often gave them out as gifts. The other Rolex model he wore was the Speedking, which was on his wrist for *The Great Escape*. The Speedking has a historical association with the military. During World War II, Rolex founder and German ex-patriot living in Switzerland, Hans Wilsdorf learned that British prisoners of war had their watches confiscated by German guards as they were being processed into the POW camps. He made the generous offer that any POW held in a camp could order and receive a Rolex of their choice and pay for it whenever they could after the war. Thousands were ordered, with more than 3,000 Rolexes going to one POW camp alone. The most popular watch requested was the Submariner.

For *The Thomas Crown Affair*, McQueen had three watches: a Patek Philippe pocket watch, a Jaeger-LeCoultre Memovox, and

> "WHY, MY WATCH IS BETTER THAN ANY OF THESE!"
>
> —STEVE MCQUEEN, UNHAPPY WITH THE PROP MASTER'S WATCH SELECTION FOR *THE THOMAS CROWN AFFAIR*

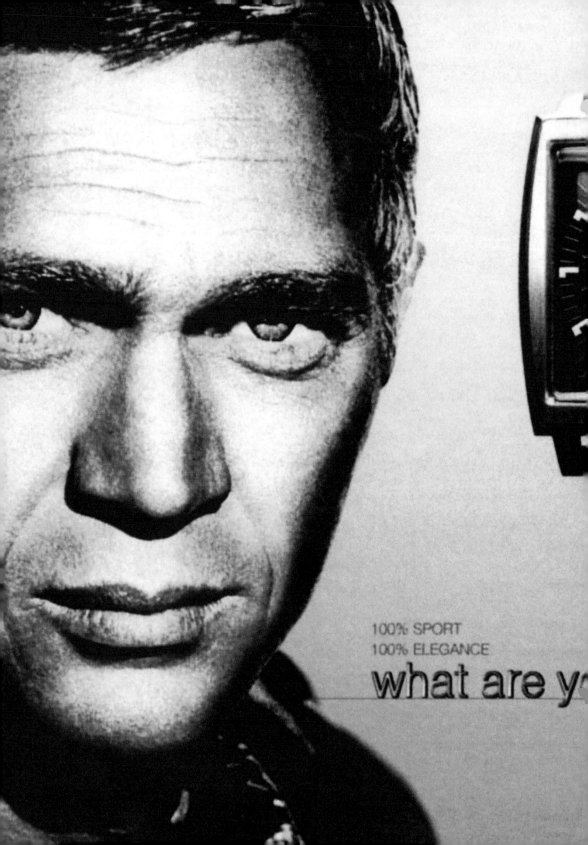

100% SPORT
100% ELEGANCE
what are y

u made of ?

a Cartier Tank. In addition to being a stately, expensive watch, the Patek Philippe thematically resonates with the scene where it appears. It has a snap lid, which means it's a hunter watch, and in that scene, Crown is overseeing his bank heist. The Cartier Tank began production right after World War I, and its design was inspired by the revolutionary Renault FT-17 tank. Numerous sites attribute the Tank worn by McQueen as being the Tank Américaine, but that model did not appear until 1989, twenty-one years after the movie. The Tank McQueen wore is likely the Cintrée.

For *Bullitt*, McQueen wore an affordable Benrus Series 3061 watch, which was the civilian version of the one used by the military during the Vietnam War.

The watch on his wrist for the International Six Days Trial in East Germany and in *The War Lover* was the German Hanhart 417ES Flyback Flieger, noted for its rugged durability. It, too, had military connections, having been supplied to the German air force and navy during World War II.

DRINKS AND DINING

THE KING OF COOL'S
COLD ONE OF CHOICE

After a hard day riding motorcycle in the desert, a day's shoot, or flying an airplane, when it came to unwinding, one thing McQueen loved was to kick back and have a cold one, or two, or . . . after all, the King of Cool answered to no one but himself.

McQueen drank a variety of beers, including Coors (at a time when it was a regional specialty), and enjoyed the regional brands whenever on location—during the shooting of *Papillion* at Jamaica, he indulged in Red Stripe so much that he gained weight, which caused the costume designers to create ever baggier prison outfits for him. McQueen's preferred beer was a working-class brew: Old Milwaukee. One restaurant he regularly patronized didn't have a beer license, so he always brought with him a six pack and had the manager put it on ice in the back. At his hangar in Santa Paula, the cooler was always filled with Old Milwaukee.

Mike Dewey, a retired movie stunt flier who gave McQueen pilot lessons, fondly remembered their after-hours sessions unwinding at the hangar, Old Milwaukee in hand. Unlike McQueen, Dewey was no fan of the beer. Reflecting on McQueen's bad-boy reputation, he joked that McQueen "was in character drinking that awful stuff."

MIXED DRINKS INSPIRED BY THE KING OF COOL

McQueen was more known for knocking back a beer than sipping a cocktail. After all, Thomas Crown was a *role*. Insofar as hard stuff was concerned, the moonshine Hilts helped make in *The Great Escape* was more in character for McQueen than a martini. Even so, that hasn't stopped mixologists from whipping up McQueen-inspired cocktails, with a number of different ones, usually tequila-based, named for him or acknowledging his reputation.

One such cocktail is the Bad Boy, a drink containing El Tesoro reposado tequila, Palo Cortado, Almacenista, Vides Emilio Lustau, Bénédictine, and mole (chocolate) bitters, with a cherry as garnish. Of it, Brian Van Flandern of Creative Cocktail Consultants said, "Steve loved good tequila and would very likely have enjoyed this cocktail."

The McQueen is another tequila cocktail. What sets it apart is that in addition to mezcal, it contains Scotch. Ingredients include Fidencio Mezcal, Glenrothes Select Scotch, dark agave syrup, a dash of orange bitters, a dash of mole bitters, and a mist of Ardbeg 10 Year, all topped with a grapefruit twist.

THE RESTAURANTS

Restaurants around the world have capitalized on the King of Cool's enduring popularity. Here's a sampling of three, two with more than a passing connection.

His link to England and racing is acknowledged in London's McQueen, "an award-winning restaurant and bar in the heart of trendy Shorditch." Inspired by the King of Cool, its décor gives numerous nods to McQueen and his roles. It's a spacious venue that includes a lounge bar, restaurant, and boutique club.

On this side of the Atlantic, there's the historic Palace Restaurant and Saloon in Prescott, Arizona. Both the town and the restaurant/bar were the location for *Junior Bonner*, and the walls contain photos and memorabilia from that movie.

A place with an even more personal connection to McQueen is One If by Land, Two If by Sea. Located in New York City's Greenwich Village, the building is historic in more ways than one. It was once a carriage house owned by vice president Aaron Burr (notoriously known for his fatal duel with treasury secretary Alexander Hamilton). The treat for McQueen fans is that the upstairs private dining area was once McQueen's apartment.

CHAPTER ELEVEN

MCQUEEN EXITS
THE LIMELIGHT

THE ECLECTIC EYE FOR AMERICANA

Once his career took off, McQueen began collecting things. This included some obvious selections—cars, motorcycles, firearms, and movie memorabilia. But over time and particularly in his reclusive later years, when he increasingly turned his back on Hollywood, his taste expanded into less expected, and in some cases head-scratching fields, and came to include tchotchkes, curios, kitsch, and in extreme cases, outright junk.

McQueen, hidden behind sunglasses and wearing a grungy hat and clothing, would happily spend the day scouring flea market stalls, rummaging for bargains. When he found something that caught his eye, he'd buy it outright or try to knock down the price. The individual behind the table rarely knew he was haggling with a living Hollywood legend who could have purchased the seller's whole inventory in a second—but what was the fun in that?

For the most part, there seemed to be no rhyme or reason to the purchases beyond simply finding a bargain. Objects ranged from the small and worthless (Kewpie dolls, fake Zippo lighters with American flags painted on them) to the big and potentially valuable (vintage gas station pumps and Wurlitzer jukeboxes).

McQueen's range of antiques included oil and electric lamps and lanterns; framed vintage needlepoint and cross-stitch embroidered samplers; old tools; milk glass shakers; metal egg baskets; vintage fans and toasters; scales; clocks for home, car, and motorcycle dealerships; tin signs for farm machinery, gasoline, motorcycles, soft drinks, and more. His furniture collection included wooden gun racks and cabinets and a kitchen cabinet and icebox. He amassed what amounted to a toy store of vintage tin toy tricycles and wagons, as well as more than ten thousand jackknives.

Two things stood out regarding this mass of material: the overwhelming majority consisted of Americana, and it largely came from a time when McQueen was young. Humble home items that were part of the tapestry of growing up can suddenly have outsized meaning to adults seeing them at flea markets. It's not unreasonable to suspect that McQueen, who was denied so much in his youth, attempted to recapture memories once held or longed for through the purchase of such items as an adult.

VINTAGE MOTORCYCLE JEWELS

At the time of his death, McQueen had one of the world's largest private motorcycle collections, counting more than two hundred bikes. Broadly speaking, McQueen's motorcycles fell into two categories: those he rode and those he collected, with some crossover between the two.

McQueen's first motorcycle was a beat-up 1946 Indian Chief with a sidecar that he bought in 1951. McQueen loved it, but the girl he was dating at the time didn't. She gave him an ultimatum—ditch the bike, or she'd walk. McQueen recalled, "Well, there was no contest. She went."

As with any serious collection, McQueen's had some real gems and included several Indian motorcycles. One classic was a 1920 Indian Powerplus Daytona Racer. In the early twentieth century, Indian, Harley-Davidson, and Excelsior were fierce competitors in the American market and rivals on the racing circuit. The Powerplus, introduced in 1916, was a 61-cubic-inch flathead twin response to the Harley-Davidson racers that had been outgunning Indian's bikes. In 1920, Indian introduced the low-riding Powerplus Daytona model that became an immediate hit with racers and one of the marque's more sought-after motorcycles in the collector's market.

Another Indian highlight in his collection was a 1934 Indian Sport Scout. Introduced in 1920, the Scout was famous for its reliability (the manufacturer's slogan was, "You can't wear out an Indian Scout"), and second only to the Indian Chief in popularity. The 1934 model was a big hit when introduced and has since become a prize among collectors.

One of the true jewels in McQueen's collection was a 1927 Indian Ace. Though the Ace Motor Company's existence was brief (1920 to 1927), it had an unmatched reputation for producing high-powered, reliable racing motorcycles. The company famously offered a $10,000 prize to any competitor who could best the motorcycle speed record of 129 miles per hour set by its XP-4 in 1923, a prize that was never claimed during the company's existence.

The Indian Motorcycle Company purchased Ace in 1927, following the founder's death. Capitalizing on the Ace name, for two years Indian produced the "Indian Ace," basically an Ace motorcycle with Indian trappings.

Indian Aces were expensive to build and only about 260 were produced in 1927. McQueen stated that Ace was his favorite marque—it was highly sought after by collectors.

An even earlier prize in McQueen's collection was the 1909 Pierce Four. George N. Pierce, a refrigerator, bird cage, and bicycle manufacturer, first produced motorcycles in 1908 as a subsidiary to his Pierce-Arrow Motor Car Company. The Pierce Four was America's first four-cylinder motorcycle and it contained several innovations that became standard in other motorcycles. Unfortunately for the company, the Pierce Four sold for less than what it cost to make it, and the company closed its doors in 1914 after producing fewer than five hundred Pierce Fours.

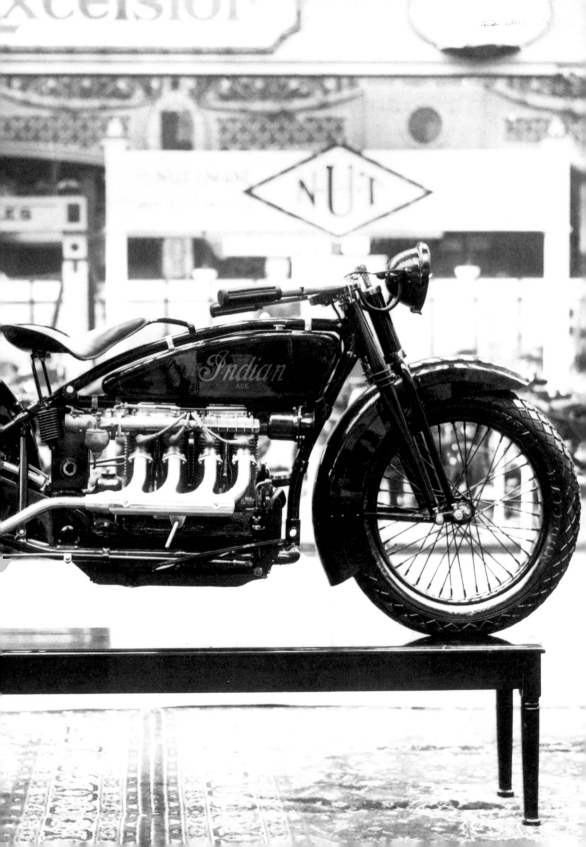

OPENING THE TREASURE CHEST

> "IN STEVE'S CASE, PERHAPS IT WAS DUE TO THE FACT HE DIDN'T HAVE ANYTHING AS A KID."
>
> —BARBARA MINTY MCQUEEN

When McQueen died in 1980, he left behind a collection that ranged from the obvious (cars and motorcycles) to the unexpected (potbellied stoves, coffee grinders, and cash registers). Four years after his death, his children decided to auction everything.

The two-day auction was held in Las Vegas, Nevada, in November 1984 and attracted more than 1,400 bidders. Highlights of the sale included the 1957 Jaguar XKSS selling for $150,000, a 1934 Packard Super 8 going for $70,000, and a 1909 Pierce motorcycle for $25,000. The Von Dutch hand-made 1905 Winton Flyer used in *The Reivers* brought in $20,000.

Even such McQueen-owned items as a bathroom toilet seat and sink went for $840. In the end, the auction raked in more than $2 million.

That auction was only the first taste of McQueen auctions to come. In 2008, his Baja Boot racer was auctioned off for $199,500. In 2011, the 1970 Porsche 911S Coupe he drove in *Le Mans* went for $1.375 million. Even mundane things, such as the corporate meeting minutes of Solar Productions, containing multiple McQueen signatures, sold for several thousand dollars. So, too, did his US Patent Office certificate for the Baja Bucket, a seat shell designed to keep motorsports drivers in place when traveling at high speeds, which he first used in his Baja Boot.

Noteworthy about that first auction, and all subsequent auctions featuring McQueen-owned items, is that all items sold at a considerable premium above similar items. The acknowledged reason was because these items once belonged to the King of Cool. One buyer at the original auction voiced an opinion shared by everyone then and since: "He was a hell of a guy, and he led the life we all wanted to lead."

THE KING OF COOL FINDS INNER PEACE

McQueen was raised Catholic. Though his disastrous childhood caused him to abandon his faith, and in many ways hardened his life, it paradoxically inspired a deep empathy for the underdog, especially disadvantaged youths. He considered his help and philanthropy a private affair, and the public only learned about his generosity after his death. McQueen's efforts ranged from such simple acts as showing up at a Los Angeles restaurant to talk to a gathering of at-risk youths (the only invited actor to do so); endowing Father Edward Wojniak's Catholic-sponsored orphanage in Taiwan; visiting and contributing money, clothing, and other items to the California Junior Boys Republic, and other philanthropic acts.

In public, he projected and perfected a "tough guy" persona that bordered on the blasphemous. At one point during the height of his fame, he was asked if he believed in God. McQueen replied, "I believe in me. God will be number one as long as I'm number one." It was a defiant statement, but hidden deep in it was a message of a longing he had yet to find: inner peace.

His journey of discovery began in 1979 after he and then-girlfriend Barbara Minty moved to Santa Paula in Ventura County, about sixty miles northwest and a world away from Los Angeles. It was, he told her, "as close to home as I can find. I want to die here."

Initially, they moved into a 3,000-square-foot airplane hangar (he later bought a nearby ranch). There, with his vast collections and the World War II–era Stearman biplane he was learning to fly, they "camped out."

Barbara later said, "It was the coolest thing ever." She recalled typical mornings where "Steve would make coffee and bring it to me, open the hangar door, and we'd watch the world from our floor-mounted bed." Then Steve would don his flying gear and take off in his Stearman.

Barbara had been raised in a religious family; in Santa Paula, she became a member of the Ventura Missionary Church and would attend service while McQueen flew his biplane. At one point after they had settled down in Santa Paula, McQueen surprised her. Barbara recalled, "One day, he walked into the hangar and out of the blue said, 'We're going to church on Sunday.'"

THE TWO FRIENDS WHO
HELPED HIM FIND GOD

Though McQueen's decision to embrace Christianity in 1979 seemed a sudden, even impulsive, choice (and one reporter's erroneously attributed to him having terminal cancer), it turned out to be one made after much serious thought and discussion over a period of years with two men, longtime close friend Pat Johnson and flight instructor Sammy Mason.

Johnson was the opposite of McQueen, a devoted husband and family man with strong religious beliefs who didn't chase women, smoke, drink, or do drugs. And he had a down-to-earth, no-nonsense toughness that McQueen respected. Over the course of their friendship, McQueen began to ask Johnson about his faith. Knowing that the quickest way to alienate McQueen was to preach to him, Johnson said it was up to McQueen to find his own way to God. By being patient and persistent, Johnson told McQueen, he'd one day find that connection.

McQueen's relationship with Mason began in Santa Paula after he had convinced Mason to give him flying lessons. Over the long hours spent together, a friendship developed, and the two began sharing stories of significant events in their lives, including the times they had cheated death.

When McQueen finished telling one of his personal stories, he stared at Mason and commented about the pilot's gentle but firm confidence. "There's something different about you, but I can't quite put my finger on it," he said.

Mason replied, "That's because I'm a Christian, Steve."

> "I DOUBT THAT I HAVE EVER SEEN A MAN FLOURISH WITH MORE SPIRITUAL REALITY IN SUCH A SHORT TIME."
>
> —SAMMY MASON

Talk moved on and flying lessons continued. Then came a day when McQueen asked if he could attend church with Mason and his wife, Wanda, a request they gladly accepted.

McQueen was nervous during that first visit to the Ventura Missionary Church with Barbara Minty, sitting in the back and not wanting to attract any attention. He came away comfortable with the experience. After three months of regular attendance, McQueen worked up the nerve to introduce himself to pastor Leonard DeWitt and request if they could have lunch so he could ask the minister some questions.

For a couple hours, McQueen grilled DeWitt about life and faith. When he was done, the pastor had one question for him. McQueen said, "You want to know if I've become a born-again Christian." Leaning forward, smiling, but serious, McQueen said, "When you invited people to pray with you to receive Christ, I prayed. So yes, I'm a born-again Christian."

Mason was one of many who noticed a dramatic change in McQueen after he had accepted God. He recalled, "I doubt that I have ever seen a man flourish with more spiritual reality in such a short time."

SANTA PAULA AND THE KING OF COOL'S FINAL FLIGHT

In *The Thomas Crown Affair* after Crown (McQueen) lands his glider, his girlfriend, Gwen (Astrid Heeren), asks him, "What do you have to worry about?" Crown replies, "What I want to be tomorrow." It was a movie story comment that, however inadvertently, foreshadowed real-life decisions McQueen made years later in Santa Paula.

He purchased a yellow 1935 Stearman biplane, but he needed someone to teach him to fly it. After asking around, he was told the best flying instructor was Sammy Mason. McQueen gave Mason a call. Mason turned him down flat, telling McQueen that he already had a full schedule of students and was not interested in training a novice. After he hung up, Mason's son, Pete, asked who he had talked to. The father replied, "Some actor named Steve McQueen. Do you know who he is?" The dumbstruck son called his father crazy for blowing off the biggest actor in Hollywood.

McQueen refused to quit. A couple more phone calls were made, and a couple more rejections were received. McQueen then tried a

> **"STEVE FLEW EVERY MORNING. HE LOVED IT—THIS WAS HIS CHURCH, HIS SPACE."**
>
> **—BARBARA MINTY MCQUEEN**

different approach. He said, "If you won't teach me, will you at least come look at my Stearman and see if it's a good airplane?" Mason said he would.

They met at the airport. After Mason had finished his inspection, McQueen asked what he thought. Mason replied, "It looks like a good plane, but the only way you can tell for sure whether it's good or not is to fly it." The two shook hands. Mason became McQueen's instructor.

McQueen threw himself into learning how to fly with three sessions a day, each session lasting two to three hours. Like the race car drivers and motorcycle racers he drove and rode with, he wanted to earn the respect of the pilots and mechanics at the airport and to be treated like just another pilot. And he got it. McQueen later proudly said, "Santa Paula Airport is my kind of country club."

McQueen owned a half-dozen aircraft. His collection included a second Stearman, a 1931 Pitcairn Mailwing, and a 1947 Piper J-3 Cub.

After his death from mesothelioma in 1980, his body was cremated. Following the conclusion of the memorial service held at his Santa Paula ranch, a "missing wingman" formation of seven aircraft flew overhead. In the lead was McQueen's Stearman N3188 (his number at Boys Republic), piloted by Santa Paula friend Larry Endicott, who cradled the urn containing McQueen's ashes. When the plane reached the nearby Pacific Ocean, he opened the urn and poured out the ashes. The slipstream then carried them into the wind, which further scattered his remains to the earth below and the heavens above.

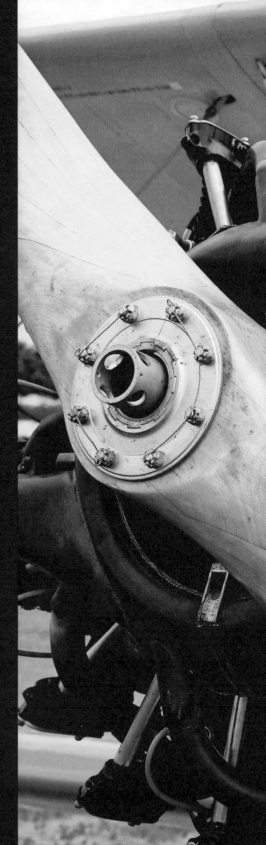

INDEX

238

PHOTO CREDITS

ALAMY: 9 (RGR Collection/Alamy Stock Photo), 14 (Science History Images/Alamy Stock Photo), 16 (ScreenProd/Photononstop/Alamy Stock Photo), 29 (AF archive/Alamy Stock Photo), 34 (Photo 12/Alamy Stock Photo), 40 (Photo 12/Alamy Stock Photo), 46 (United Archives GmbH/Alamy Stock Photo), 47 (Entertainment Pictures/Alamy Stock Photo), 48 (Moviestore collection Ltd/Alamy Stock Photo), 54 (Pictorial Press Ltd/Alamy Stock Photo), 58 (AF archive/Alamy Stock Photo), 64 (United Archives GmbH/Alamy Stock Photo), 67 (Trinity Mirror/Mirrorpix/Alamy Stock Photo), 70 (Collection Christophel/Alamy Stock Photo), 72 (AF archive/Alamy Stock Photo), 75 (Pictorial Press Ltd/Alamy Stock Photo), 78 (Photo 12/Alamy Stock Photo), 79 (United Archives GmbH/Alamy Stock Photo), 82 (AF archive/Alamy Stock Photo), 85 (AF archive/Alamy Stock Photo), 86 (Moviestore collection Ltd/Alamy Stock Photo), 92 (AF archive/Alamy Stock Photo), 95 (Pictorial Press Ltd/Alamy Stock Photo), 96 (MIRISCH CORPORATION/Ronald Grant Archive/Alamy Stock Photo), 98 (ScreenProd/Photononstop/Alamy Stock Photo), 104 (AF archive/Alamy Stock Photo), 105 (colaimages/Alamy Stock Photo), 110 (ScreenProd/Photononstop/Alamy Stock Photo), 112 (Photo 12/Alamy Stock Photo), 114 (United Archives GmbH/Alamy Stock Photo), 115 (ScreenProd/Photononstop/Alamy Stock Photo), 116 (ScreenProd/Photononstop/Alamy Stock Photo), 119 (Moviestore collection Ltd/Alamy Stock Photo), 123 (ScreenProd/Photononstop/Alamy Stock Photo), 126 (ScreenProd/Photononstop/Alamy Stock Photo), 128 (ScreenProd/Photononstop/Alamy Stock Photo), 130 (Trinity Mirror/Mirrorpix/Alamy Stock Photo), 131 (Moviestore collection Ltd/Alamy Stock Photo), 132 (Collection Christophel/Alamy Stock Photo), 134-135 (United Archives GmbH/Alamy Stock Photo), 136 (Ronald Grant Archive/Alamy Stock Photo), 137 (Keystone Pictures USA/Alamy Stock Photo), 138 (United Archives GmbH/Alamy Stock Photo), 141 (United Archives GmbH/Alamy Stock Photo), 142 (ScreenProd/Photononstop/Alamy Stock Photo), 144 (Everett Collection, Inc./Alamy Stock Photo), 149 (Moviestore collection Ltd/Alamy Stock Photo) 152 (Pictorial Press Ltd/Alamy Stock Photo), 154 (dpa picture alliance/Alamy Stock Photo), 155 (dpa picture alliance/Alamy Stock Photo), 156 (United Archives GmbH/Alamy Stock Photo), 157 (INTERFOTO/Alamy Stock Photo), 160 (ZUMA Press, Inc./Alamy Stock Photo), 163 (ScreenProd/Photononstop/Alamy Stock Photo), 166 (ScreenProd/Photononstop/Alamy Stock Photo), 167 (Everett Collection Historical/Alamy Stock Photo), 173 (Pictorial Press Ltd/Alamy Stock Photo), 184 (Pictorial Press Ltd/Alamy Stock Photo), 192 (United Archives GmbH/Alamy Stock Photo), 195 (Photo 12/Alamy Stock Photo), 198 (Trinity Mirror/Mirrorpix/Alamy Stock Photo), 205 (ScreenProd/Photononstop/Alamy Stock Photo), 206 (The Advertising Archives/Alamy Stock Photo), 219 (Heritage Image Partnership Ltd/Alamy Stock Photo), 236 (Herb Quick/Alamy Stock Photo)

ANDRES REYNAGA/MCQUEEN: 214

EDWARD QUINN: 159

FREE VINTAGE POSTERS: 4, 30

GETTY: front endpages (Henri Bureau), 5 (Movie Poster Image Art), 6 (John Dominis), 10 (John Dominis), 17 (Henri Bureau), 18 (CBS Photo Archive), 21 (Jack Mitchell), 22 (Three Lions), 25 (Bettmann), 26 (Silver Screen Collection), 33 (MGM Studios), 36 (CBS Photo Archive), 39 (CBS Photo Archive), 42 (CBS Photo Archive), 44 (CBS Photo Archive), 45 (John Dominis), 50 (John Dominis), 53 (Sunset Boulevard), 56 (Archive Photos), 61 (John Dominis), 62 (John Dominis), 68 (Jimmy Sime), 76 (Silver Screen Collection), 81 (John Dominis), 84 (Movie Poster Image Art), 89 (Sunset Boulevard), 90 (Bettmann), 100 (The Enthusiast Network), 101 (The Enthusiast Network), 102 (Michael Ochs Archives), 106 (John Dominis), 108 (Movie Poster Image Art), 120 (CBS Photo Archive), 124 (Cinerama), 143 (Sunset Boulevard), 146 (DESCAMPS Michel), 150 (CBS Photo Archive), 151 (CBS Photo Archive), 164 (Stanley Bielecki Movie Collection), 168 (Movie Poster Image Art), 176-177 (John Dominis), 178 (John Dominis), 180 (John Dominis), 181 (John Dominis), 182 (John Dominis), 186 (John Dominis), 187 (John Dominis), 188 (John Dominis), 189 (John Dominis), 191 (Silver Screen Collection), 196 (AFP), 200-201 (John Dominis), 202 (John Dominis), 208 (Ralph Crane), 210 (Silver Screen Collection), 211 (Paul Popper/Popperfoto), 212 (Silver Screen Collection), 220 (Heritage Images), 222 (Topical Press Agency), 225 (Christopher Furlong), 226 (John Dominis), 228 (John Dominis), 234 (Bettmann), back endpages (John Dominis)

LIBRARY OF CONGRESS: 13, 231, 232

MATT STONE: 113, 174

MOTORTREND/THE ENTHUSIAST NETWORK: 216